All the restaurants and pubs in this book are considered to be of a sufficiently-decent standard to warrant a visit. Particularly good places are marked with one ★, outstandingly good ones get two ★ ★. The ratings were decided after independent inspections. No establishment pays to be included and no advertising is accepted.

All the information was correct at the time of going to print but the restaurant world is in a constant state of flux and readers are always advised to check first before setting out.

EATING OUT

IN BIRMINGHAM AND THE MIDLANDS

Including Stratford-upon-Avon and the Cotswolds

by Alison Davison
of The Birmingham Post

ACKNOWLEDGEMENTS

My grateful thanks go to The Birmingham Post as well as Mandy McGeever, Poppy Brady, Mary Munford, Jayne Howarth, Warren Smith, Richard Binns and Shaun Hill for their kindness and know-how, and Julian for his constant willingness to eat meat on my behalf.

For Laurie and Amelia,
again and always

Text © Alison Davison
All rights reserved

Published by Alison Davison 2005.
PO Box 7283, Stourbridge, DY8 2ZR.
Email info@eat-the-midlands.co.uk

First published in 2001. Revised June 2002.

ISBN 0-9551320-0-2

Typesetting and design by Warren Smith.
Printed by Technique Studios, Banbury, Oxon.

CONTENTS

INTRODUCTION

It's been four years since the first edition of Eating Out in Birmingham and the Midlands appeared. I commented back then about the revolution taking place in the region and there's been no let-up in the pace of change since.

The best news of all was when Birmingham finally staked its place on the culinary map by winning two Michelin stars at the beginning of 2005 - one for Jessica's and one for Simpsons. It's not that Michelin stars are the be-all and end-all but more that they brought publicity and recognition finally to a city that had been the butt of too many jokes and which has strived beyond belief to rejuvenate itself.

Eating out, though, is rarely about 'fine dining' - that deadly phrase can too often make the heart sink. The whole range of dining in the region continues to improve across the board.

In Brum. new arrivals such as Prana and Opus in the city offer real style as well as great food. Quality gastropubs are popping up all over the place, a substantial number thanks to the prolific collaboration between Paul Hales, Paul Salisbury and M&B.

This boom isn't just down to entrepreneurs. Some serious chefs have also decided pubs are the way ahead - witness Steve Love at the College Arms near Stratford, Ian Wallace at the Wykham Arms near Banbury and Roger Narbett of the Chequers and Bell and Cross, both in Worcestershire.

The centre of Birmingham still has a dearth of decent food pubs but hungry shoppers are benefiting from the city's reinvention of itself as a retail paradise. Not only did Selfridges, for example, actually make Brum seem cool, it also brought a great food hall with excellent places to eat (as well as a classy restaurant).

Equally, the World of Food at House of Fraser offers a fantastic range of quality places to eat and decent cafes, once such a rarity, have appeared, from the Eat chain to Café Paxton at the Paxton & Whitfield cheese shop.

Of course, there have been some sad departures along the way, most notably the Merchant House in Ludlow. At the time of writing, its chef-patron Shaun Hill was still hoping to open a place nearer Birmingham but his hopes were receding as the months went by. At least it gave him the time to write his foreword....thank you Shaun.

Here's to great food at good prices. Happy eating!

Alison Davison

FOREWORD

by Shaun Hill

There is a choice of good restaurants in the Midlands. It wasn't always possible to make this claim but it certainly is now. More important, there are places that derive from and are a celebration of the Midlands and not just offshoots of London restaurants being cynically rolled out for the provincial market.

In the past, large cities like Birmingham have lagged behind the rest of the region. Good ethnic eateries plus a sprinkling of dull, pricey and posh spots for businessmen were the best of what was on offer. The impression was always that urban Midlanders preferred to drive out of town to eat anyway. So the Warwickshire countryside would have more choice than the city centre.

The majority of these destinations were housed in hotels rather than standing alone as restaurants. And there can be a distinct difference between the two. A hotel provides food alongside clean bed linen and - usually - nice views, principally as a service to resident guests. In a restaurant, the meal is the whole point so all the efforts are concentrated on getting the food and buzz right and no amount of spacious bathroom or complimentary morning newspapers will save them if they do not. The upsurge in restaurants and even hotel restaurants that can claim a distinct and separate identity is evidence that times have changed

There was always fine produce in our region, the best butchers in Britain, fruit and vegetables from the Vale of Evesham, good lines of supply to fishing ports around the country. There was also always the talent. All that was missing was the entrepreneurial skill to open the sort of places that we might want to eat in so that this talent and ingredient would be showcased.

The point of this guide is to let you navigate not only towards the good and the fairly priced but also to give some clue as to style. The right place to meet your new in-laws may not be the same place needed to please a foodie friend or mollify a disgruntled partner. It's as important to the restaurant trade that the great places prosper and poor places close as it is to the diner. Better eating for us all.

FAVOURITES

Everyone has their own preferences but here are mine.

Indian

Bilash, Wolverhampton

Lasan, Birmingham

Blue Mango, Birmingham

Mokhams, Birmingham

Chinese/oriental

Wongs, Birmingham

Wing Wah, Birmingham

Ruby's, Bearwood

China Red, Birmingham

Wagamama, Birmingham

Gourmet experience

Le Champignon Sauvage, Cheltenham

Restaurant Sat Bains, Nottingham

Hibiscus, Ludlow

Simpsons, Birmingham

Jessica's, Birmingham

Mr Underhill's, Ludlow

Lords of the Manor, Glos

Food pubs

Waterdine, Llanfair Waterdine

Stagg, Titley

Crabmill, Preston Bagot

Bell and Cross, Clent

College Arms, nr Stratford

Three Crowns, Ullingswick

Wykham Arms, Oxon

Bell, Tanworth-in-Arden

Howard Arms, Ilmington

Vegetarian

Edmunds, Henley-in-Arden (not a dedicated vegetarian restaurant but fab nevertheless)

Sibila's at Body and Being, Birmingham

Jyoti, Birmingham

ABBERLEY

Elms Hotel ★

Fine Dining

Stockton Road, Abberley, Worcs, WR6 6AT.
www.theelmshotel.co.uk
01299 896666.

Abberley is a particularly lovely part of Worcestershire and the Elms hotel is the sort of grand historic building which regularly appears in BBC costume dramas as some old fogey's country pile.

It's owned by the von Essen group, so you can imagine the sort of oak-panelled, soft-carpeted world you're in.

Despite its popularity as a wedding venue, it's still worth seeking out when you're in need of a treat, with calm, solicitous service and great cooking. The Brooke restaurant is spacious, chintzy and comfortable.

The food is truly excellent and not at all badly priced for the quality, with dishes that combine good flavours effortlessly well, cooked with precision and talent.

If the weather's good, see if you can eat outside - the grounds are a delight and the views wonderful.

ACTON TRUSSELL

Moat House

Modern British

Lower Penkridge Road, Acton Trussell,
Staffordshire, ST17 0RJ.
www.moathouse.co.uk
01785 712217. Fax 01785 715344.

A charming listed building with not just a moat but also a canal to give it that special occasion waterside feel.

Staffordshire doesn't have too much to shout about when it comes to food but the Moat House obviously aims to fill that gap and proudly proclaims itself the county's premier hotel.

The restaurant - in an enormous conservatory, not the most practical place for a dining room - is traditional in style and outlook.

The food goes for the upmarket feel with a choice of menus including a gourmet tasting selection. All generally pleasant enough but you may feel it doesn't quite justify its self-confidence.

ALCESTER HEATH

Fusion

Modern European

Longbarn Village, Alcester Heath, Alcester, Warks, B49 5JJ.
www.fusionbrasserie.com
01789 762000.

A très chic place in the très chic little gathering that is Longbarn village - a collection of upmarket shops and this restaurant in a gathering of barn conversions, all very tastefully done.

The food is mainly Italian but there's also a collection of other dishes too, from rack of lamb perhaps to sausage and mash.

It's not 100 per cent there but some dishes, especially a Dover sole, were spot-on. A very friendly place which is trying hard.

ALDERMINSTER

The Bell

Pubs/bars

**Alderminster, nr Stratford-upon-Avon,
Warwickshire, CV37 8NY.**
www.thebellald.co.uk
01789 450414.

A genteel, sedate and reliable place just outside Stratford, the Bell is not the place for those looking for cutting edge decor or übertrendy fare.

But it has a lot to offer nonetheless, including some temptingly homemade dishes, a restful ambience and thoughtful, non-intrusive service.

The vegetarian dishes are inventive and there's clearly a strong emphasis on quality, from excellent soufflés to meltingly-soft lamb shank and well-cooked fish.

Ettington Park Hotel

Fine dining

**Alderminster, near Stratford-upon-Avon,
Warks, CV37 8BU.**
www.handpicked.co.uk
01789 450123.

Forty acres of beautiful grounds including a ruined 12th century church surround Ettington Park Hotel, an immense gothic pile just outside Stratford. It's not surprising that the place abounds with tales of ghostly goings-on within its ornate historic walls.

But it doesn't just have to be for American tourists. A fair share of celebrity guests stay here (the NEC isn't far) too and it's perfect for the country house hotel-loving crowd.

There are tables on the terrace so you can enjoy a sunlit gin and tonic on a lovely evening or perhaps a leisurely sunny lunch.

Service is careful and polite and the food on offer in the formal, rather hushed dining room is cooking in the grand hotel style - generally textbook, gracious stuff, elaborately presented and designed as much to fulfil expectations as to tickle the tastebuds.

Prices match the grandeur of the building.

ALVESTON

Baraset Barn★

Pubs/bars

**1 Pimlico Lane, Alveston,
near Stratford-upon-Avon, CV37 7RJ.
www.barasetbarn.co.uk
01789 295510.**

Baraset Barn Country Bar and Grill is another addition to the Paul Hales/Paul Salisbury empire (the Boot, Crabmill, Orange Tree et al) and the swankiest one yet.

The place spent some time as Pimlicos, an Italian restaurant, and was stylish enough then but is even more so now.

Big sofas fill the orangery bar area (yes, you can just come here for a drink, it's OK), white granite-topped tables, lots of oak and swish seating create an impressive yet still comfortable dining room

The food is as no-nonsense and appealing as ever - pizzas, pastas, grills, lots of fish, salads. Not that they're all the bog standard norm by any means. The pasta dishes include lobster ravioli and an upmarket macaroni cheese with gorgonzola, ricotta and baby spinach while the fish section has more lobster (grilled, with chips), sole meunière and a platter of fruits de mer.

Definitely pub eating at the premiership level.

ARDENS GRAFTON

Golden Cross

Pubs/bars

**Wixford Road, Ardens Grafton, Alcester,
Warks, B50 4LG.
01789 772420.**

It's worth getting a large scale map to track down Ardens
Grafton and the Golden Cross. But once you find it (and
that can take some doing - look a few miles outside Alcester
or Bidford-on-Avon), you'll understand what I mean.

Not only is it a lovely pastoral spot, with great views
across several counties, but the pub is a feelgood place
and very friendly for all its gastro ambitions. Witness the
presence of locals who just pop in just for a drink (gasp)
and the sound of children in the pub garden.

The food's good too, regular bistro stuff (moules marinière,
chicken breast in garlic and wild mushroom sauce) mixed
up with the odd retro item, such as prawn cocktail Taj
Mahal and T-bone steak with tomato, mushroom, onion
rings and chips (that's chips, notice, not fries). Crowd-
pleasers, in other words.

It's the sort of unpretentious, easy-going place you'd make
a regular date with.

*Before you criticise
someone, you should walk
a mile in their shoes.
That way, when you criticise them,
you are a mile away from them
and you have their shoes."*

Frieda Norris

ARMSCOTE

Fox and Goose

Pubs/bars

**Armscote, Stratford-upon-Avon, CV37 8DD.
01608 682293.**

Youthful, trendy things go on inside this redbrick village pub not far from Bardsville. Stripped wooden floors and old pine tables give a nicely rustic backdrop to its foodie ambitions.

The tempting selection chalked up on the blackboard travels the world in style, from maybe gravadlax with blinis to lamb koftas.

The atmosphere is buzzy - it's popular and understandably so as hearty, quality food is reliably on the cards. Classics often get a twist.

ASTON CANTLOW

King's Head

Pubs/bars

**Bearley Road, Aston Cantlow,
near Stratford-upon-Avon, Warks, B95 6HY.
www.thekingsheadatastoncantlow.co.uk
01789 488242.**

This popular country pub regularly packs them in, especially at weekends, when booking is essential.

The village of Aston Cantlow is very pretty and the pub is well-placed within it, right next to the very scenic church. It is, famously, the place where William Shakespeare's parents were married and just one mile from Mary Arden's house.

The interior is beautifully done out with a carefully-designed modern rustic look to go with the flagstoned floors and original beams. There's a pretty garden too.

AYMESTREY

The Riverside Inn

Pubs/bars

Aymestrey, Herefordshire, HR6 9ST.
www.theriversideinn.org
01568 708440.

A cosy and homely, old-fashioned pub (more than 400 years old) which serves masses of homemade, freshly-prepared dishes.

The menu is ambitious and although not every flavour combination may quite come off, its ambitions are laudable. Good veggie choice too.

The spot - on the bank of the Lugg - is idyllic and the area is great for a trip out, with the Mortimer Trail and various gardens and heritage sites within reach.

BALSALL COMMON

Haigs Hotel

Modern British

273 Kenilworth Road, Balsall Common,
near Coventry, CV7 7EL.
www.haigshotel.co.uk
01676 533004.

Within this smalish and rather ordinary-looking hotel, there is an ambitious restaurant offering upmarket and good value food.

There may be pan-seared scallops with pea puree and lemon oil (very good) to start with, or smoked salmon on a buckwheat blini with creme fraiche and Sevruga caviar.

Expect similarly-upmarket brasserie fare among the main courses, such as calves' liver or rump of spring lamb among the mains.

Not everything quite hits the mark but it's a homely, friendly place and they are clearly very proud of sous chef Jenny Goff who won the Coventry Chef of the Year title in 2005.

BANBURY

Hyltons

Modern British

27 Parsons Street, Banbury, OX16 5LY.
01295 270777.

Hylton's is a revelation - it's a smart, smallish place with just two in the kitchen but it turns out great, fresh food at bargain prices - especially at lunchtime.

Midday, two courses cost just £7.95 and three £10.95 and for that, the choice may include ambitious and quality fare such a slow-roast tournedos of gammon or grilled salmon fillet on courgette ribbons with tomato and chive velouté.

Definitely one to bear in mind when in that neck of the woods...

The finest landscape in the world is improved by a good inn in the foreground.

Samuel Johnson

BARNT GREEN

Barnt Green Inn

Pubs/bars

**22 Kendal End Road, Barnt Green,
Birmingham, B45 8PZ.
www.barntgreeninn.co.uk
0121 445 4949.**

Another chic gastropub from Pauls Salisbury and Hales in conjunction with M&B. This is a big, big place and has left its grim history behind with an incredibly stylish revamp.

The food, as always with their ventures, is simple yet sophisticated and reliably good quality. Staff are young and matey and the place has a real buzz.

Try the grazing tables with their high stools if you fancy going up in the world...

BEAMHURST

Restaurant Gilmore at Strine's Farm ★

Modern British

**Beamhurst, Uttoxeter, Staffordshire, ST14 5DZ.
www.restaurantgilmore.com
01889 507100.**

If you ever wondered what became of Paul Gilmore - who used to have an eponymous restaurant in Hockley - here's your answer.

In a comfortable farmhouse (his home) in a beautiful rural spot, he has created a new, smart yet homely small restaurant. And the food is simply wonderful.

There's good use of local produce and his cooking is as skillful as ever. It's good value too, at £27.50 for three courses. A delight.

BEARWOOD

Azzari Too

Global

204 Lightwoods Road, Bearwood,
Warley, B67 5AZ.
www.azzaritoo.co.uk
0121 429 6621.

You couldn't get much more suburban than this place, nestling on a corner of downtown Bearwood, just a few steps away from the busy high street (and the Bear pub) and rows of houses stretching away in every other direction.

The canopied, cream exterior, neatly bordered by green hedging, is matched by a calm cream interior, a subtly pleasant backdrop for surprisingly global food.

Gnocchi, pasta, roast rib of beef with horseradish, coconut curry, halloumi, Malaysian laksa chicken - all these and more can make an appearance and jolly robust most of it is too. Friendly stuff and proud of it.

BELBROUGHTON

The Queens

Pubs/bars

Queens Hill, Belbroughton, DY9 0DU.
www.the-queens.co.uk
01562 730973.

A village as pretty as Belbroughton deserves a pub as pretty as the Queens - creeper-covered, elegant, all overflowing window boxes and parasol-topped tables topped with old champagne bottles holding fresh flowers.

Happily, the food is as hale and hearty as required and varied enough to suit all tastes.

Everything is homemade and the place gets packed with locals and visitors from further afield.

BERKSWELL

Nailcote Hall

Fine dining

The Oak Room restaurant, Nailcote Lane, Berkswell, Warks, CV7 7DE.
www.nailcotehall.co.uk
02476 466174.

Nailcote Hall is a stately and impressive black and white place in 15 acres of grounds and its Oak Room restaurant is just one of the attractions on offer - the place is also a hotel/cabaret venue/golf and country club.

Soft lights, beams, polished mahogany tables and silverware all speak romance and opulence - in discreetly hushed tones, of course.

Not a cheap place but the food is impressive and as opulent and well-presented as the surroundings. Indeed, some of the desserts could qualify as modern art.

The age of your children is a key factor in how quickly you are served in a restaurant. We once had a waiter in Canada who said, 'Could I get you your check?' and we answered, 'How about the menu first?'

Erma Bombeck

Al Frash

Pakistani

186 Ladypool Road, Sparkbrook, B12 8JS.
0121 753 3120.

Al-Frash, in the heart of Birmingham's balti belt, is a goodie - brighter-looking than most and very welcoming and professional.

Having won several top balti awards, it's understandably always busy.

It's bring your own of course, which makes it even more of a bargain. Spicing is careful and the food tastes reassuringly fresh.

All Bar One

Pubs/bars

The Water's Edge, Brindleyplace
and Newhall Street, city centre.
www.mbplc.com
0121 644 5861 and
0121 212 9991 respectively.

All Bar One is a chain but decent enough for all that.

The trendily-basic bars have lots of bare wood (floors, tables, even old church seats), young staff and a blackboard of food which can seem something of a lower priority to the buzz of people enjoying a drink in the laidback, no-fuss surroundings.

The reasonably-priced filling food helps to soak up some of the alcohol.

Worth a visit for the feelgood ambience.

Apres

Pubs/bars

Summer Row, Birmingham, B3 1JJ.
www.summerrow.com
0121 212 1661.

Apres is a buzzy, modern bar within the smart newish Summer Row development.

Youthful and lively, the atmosphere is definitely more bar than restaurant but the food, although simple and comforting (jacket potatoes, pizzas, paninis et al) is well done and hits the spot.

There are big screens here showing sports events, and it can get a bit smoky - and noisy - but it's clearly a hit.

Aria restaurant at the Hyatt Regency Hotel

Modern British

2 Bridge Street, city centre, B1 2JZ.
www.birmingham.regency.hyatt.com
0121 643 1234.

In October 2004, some £4 million was spent on revamping the Hyatt's restaurant, bar and meeting rooms.

The restaurant, now called Aria, occupies the wide open prairie that is the hotel lobby but better lighting and use of space makes it rather more intimate than previously.

It's all very swish and comfortable - and perfect for Symphony Hall or the Rep - but the high-ish prices aren't always justified by what's on the plate.

On the right lines but still room for improvement.

Arts Cafe,
St Martins Church

Modern British

St Martins Church, Bullring, Birmingham.

If 'church cafe' makes you think of polystyrene cups and plastic tablecloths, pay this place a visit.

The Arts Cafe attached to St Martins - which makes such a fantastic centrepiece for the Bullring - is smart and ultramodern. Happily, its contemporary furnishings blend well with its ancient setting.

The food is just as up-to-the-minute as the look with tapas and hearty, good quality main courses such as lamb's liver with roast garlic mash providing excellent value.

It's the perfect stopping-off place for the weary shopper but be warned - it does get busy and you may have to queue.

Bank

Modern British

4 Brindleyplace, Birmingham. B1 2JB.
www.bankrestaurants.com
0121 633 4466.

A big, ultra-modern eaterie, the service from the Mao-suited, professional staff is slick, the food spot-on and the experience buzzy.

It can get noisy but it's an impressively good place to eat all the same.

The food covers an excellent range of cuisines and price levels, from seared, oriental-flavoured tuna to excellent fish and chips and from confit duck leg with sautéed potatoes and sauce vierge to roast quail with wild mushroom and herb risotto.

A favourite for business lunches.

Bar Epernay

Pubs/bars

The Mailbox, Birmingham, B1 1RF.
www.utopiainns.co.uk
0121 632 1430.

A Champagne and piano bar, no less, that aims squarely for the new Birmingham wealthy, Bar Epernay has decent standards too when it comes to food and sets its store by quality sourcing.

The interior is modern but not so cool it hurts. A circular fireplace and bubbling water walls are impressive but the centre of attention is the shiny black grand piano which sits on a revolving podium by the window. Rumour has it you can drop your requests into a top hat for the pianist to attempt.

In this comfy, laidback place, the Champagne list provides the usual big-name suspects, including Taittinger, Roederer and Dom Perignon, with two house versions, Moet and Beaumont de Crayeres.

Alongside is simple but good brasserie-style fodder. There are specials and snacks as well as the à la carte, which offers starters such as Morecambe Bay potted shrimps and charcuterie while mains include perhaps Aberdeenshire beef tournedos, roast corn-fed chicken or rack of Cornish lamb.

Bar Estilo

Spanish

The Mailbox, Birmingham, B1 1RF.
www.barestilo.co.uk
0121 643 3443.

A Spanish-themed bar and restaurant very popular with families. Lotsa tapas but if you're looking for the authentic chilled fino experience, this probably isn't the place for you.

Still, the food isn't likely to make any enemies and includes a varied selection - including burgers and sausage and mash - for those in a non-Spanish mood. Very child-friendly and a relaxed, feelgood place.

Barajee

Indian

265 Broad Street, Birmingham, B1 2DS.
www.restaurantbarajee.com
0121 643 6700.

This sibling for the Rajnagar in Olton, Solihull, has landed in an excellent Broad Street spot.

Up on the first floor, there are fine views of the Gas Street canal basin (so much better than it sounds) and some pretty good Indian food.

It's aiming upmarket, so expect a bit of wannabe swanky decor here and there but basically it's just a jolly competent eaterie with lots of satisfying dishes on hand to jolly along the world weary.

Bartons Arms

Thai

144 High Street, Aston, Birmingham B6 4UP.
www.bartons-arms.co.uk
0121 335 5988.

This astonishing Victorian pub - a temple to the ornate art of the tiler - was being left to rot until the present owners, Oakham Ales, stepped in.

And the surprises don't stop there. The historic pub now specialises in Thai food and has three Thai chefs hard at work in the busy kitchen turning out a droolingly-wide range of delicious dishes at great prices.

There are some wonderful beers on offer too. A rather strange but happy experience.

Berlioz

Modern British

**Burlington Hotel, Burlington Arcade,
126 New Street, B2 4JQ.
www.burlingtonhotel.com
0121 633 1737.**

The comfortable, upholstered chairs, formally-draped tables and dramatically-curtained tall windows at Berlioz all speak well-to-do hotel.

Service is formal and efficient without being stiff and the food is generally very good. The menu is international with no fear of surprisingly exotic combinations but the spicing and mixing of flavours are deft and well-balanced. An appealing mix.

Puddings are as indulgent as any sugar-craver could wish.

Blue Mango

Indian

**5 Regency Wharf, Gas Street Basin,
Birmingham, B1 2DS.
www.bluemangorestaurants.co.uk
0121 633 4422.**

This great new Indian restaurant tucked just off Broad Street offers a sleek, modern decor and great food.

Upstairs is its sibling Jimmy Spices, a buffet set-up offering Thai, Indian, Chinese and even Italian dishes.

Downstairs, the emphasis is on Indian and though the occasional global influence - a touch of balsamic here, a tomato olive salsa there - creeps in, the effect adds to rather than detracts from some imaginative culinary thinking.

There are traditional as well as more unusual dishes but everything is treated with care and attention to detail. Definitely worth a visit.

Buonissimo

Italian

1 Albany Road, Harborne, B17 9JX.
0121 426 2444.

Bustling little Buonissimo has built up a regular local trade with its easy-living food served up in smart yet relaxed, youthful surroundings.

With its white walls, glass shelves, spotlights and mirrors, it offers a modernist, feelgood café space with food that's informal and out to satisfy rather than impress.

It also gets away from that osso-bucco stereotype of Italian restaurant food with tempting dishes such as risottos with saffroned onions, aubergine and rocket or lemon and basil-marinated chicken breast with a crisp salad.

Cafe Ikon

Spanish

The Ikon Gallery, 1 Oozells Square,
Brindleyplace, B1 2HS.
www.ikon-gallery.co.uk
0121 248 3226.

A favourite tapas place, this bijou place in the cutting edge Ikon Gallery has great style - white, modern, simple lines but with lots of clever touches to make the place feel beautifully comfortable and vibrant.

The food hits the same happy blend of trendy and fun and is simply made for sharing.

If you aren't in the mood for lots of nibbles, go straight for the paellas, of which there are several versions available, including vegetarian.

Cafe Lazeez

Indian

**116 Wharfside Street, the Mailbox,
Birmingham, B1 1RF.
www.cafelazeez.co.uk
0121 643 7979.**

This is Indian food contemporary style, with looks and prices to match.

The dishes are good and clearly fresh, if fearsomely spicy in parts (and of course, you never know which parts until you take a mouthful).

This is the first Cafe Lazeez outside London and its metropolitan ideas include a discretionary 12.5 per cent service, unisex loos and a charge for the rather good chutneys put on the table with your popadoms.

Cafe Paxton

Modern British

**Paxton & Whitfield, the Mailbox, B1 1XL.
www.paxtonandwhitfield.co.uk
0121 632 1440.**

The wonderful cheesemongers Paxton & Whitfield have added another string to their bow with this smart modern cafe attached to their shop in the Mailbox.

As you'd expect, cheese features heavily in the choice of cooked dishes, sandwiches and soups on offer but the selection doesn't seem out of kilter.

Indeed, this is seriously tempting stuff with excellent risottos (enriched with two cheeses) and hearty, flavoursome gratins.

Service was off the boil during an inspection visit but it wasn't enough to spoil a very pleasant and relaxed meal.

Cafe Soya

Oriental

Cathay Street, Arcadian Centre, Birmingham, B5 4TD.
0121 683 8350.

A bright and busy caff serving bargain and very good oriental food from Vietnam, Thailand and China.

It's all pretty basic but it's excellent quality (especially at these prices) and there's an authentic buzz to the place. Be warned - it does get extremely busy.

Unlicensed but with a wide range of soft drinks.

Café Soya was due to move to larger premises nearby late in 2005.

Cathay

Chinese

86 Holloway Head, Birmingham, B1 1NB.
0121 666 7788.

This oriental restaurant is a stunner - both in strikingly modern looks and in cuisine.

Half of the menu in this pale wood, stylish eaterie is zippily fresh, luxurious but quite straightforward fare - predominantly fish and seafood but with some meat and poultry thrown in.

The other half - the "specialist vegetarian food" - is positively bewildering. Here we have veggie dishes, made from presumably some sort of oriental Quorn, that exactly ape carnivorous classics - there are veggie king prawns, Vietnamese pork, Cathay duck, shark fin soup ... the list is enormous (nine starters, four entrees, 13 main courses).

The non-veggie dishes seem guaranteed to please but the vegetarian jury's still out on their "So" counterparts.

An all-you-can-eat buffet style now dominates.

Chez Amis

Modern European

**7 Fletchers Walk, Paradise Circus,
Birmingham, B3 3HJ.
0121 233 1533.**

Chez Amis, tucked away in the bowels of Paradise Circus, was once known as Casa Paco, a homely, down-to-earth Spanish restaurant.

It's now under different ownership and is a homely, down-to-earth Spanish and French restaurant.

Not much has changed, in other words, apart from the addition of some French dishes to an otherwise very similar, eclectic menu.

The decor may be all a bit 70s with its artex and wrought iron but the food is great - good quality, unpretentious and well-priced.

Try one of the paellas or tuck into some excellently-cooked fresh fish. There's also a fixed price menu offering even better value.

China Red

Chinese

**193 Broad Street, Birmingham, B15 1AY.
0121 632 6688.**

New Chinese restaurants can be a bit of a rarity with the onslaught of Thai, Japanese and the ubiquitous 'modern British'. But if they're as good as China Red, a recent arrival on buzzing Broad Street, they're more than welcome.

It's a big place but has lots of friendly staff to cope. Despite the rather snazzily up-to-date interior, the menu is mostly traditional Cantonese but everything is done very well.

Pork and prawn dumplings are tastier than their anaemic appearance would initially suggest while the spare ribs are messily gorgeous. But star dish of the review night was a tender and succulent chicken satay.

Chung Ying

Chinese

16-18 Wrottesley Street, Birmingham, B5 4RT.
www.chungying.co.uk
0121 622 5669.

The old Brummie favourite may face a lot of eastern competition these days but it remains the Chinese of choice for many.

It occupies an imposing corner building in Chinatown and covers two large floors - a huge amount of space, a huge number of diners (and it nearly always seems full) and a menu listing at least 300 dishes.

Some dishes may seem quite fatty but may still be deeply, unctuously flavoursome. It's very sociable food of course and this is a very business-like environment (which can get smoky).

Chung Ying Garden

Chinese

17 Thorp Street, city centre, B5 4AT.
www.chungying.co.uk
0121 666 6622.

This little sister to the mighty Chung Ying was opened back in 1987 and is big enough to host several office parties all at the same time, upstairs and downstairs.

At full throttle, this place can seat more than 350 people and the upstairs has karaoke facilities.

Still, CYG has that lavish style you'd expect in the middle of Chinatown and the lavish choice to go with it.

Alcohol is a misunderstood vitamin.

P G Wodehouse

Cielo

Italian

6 Brindleyplace, Birmingham, B1 2JB.
www.cielobirmingham.com
0121 632 6882.

Spacious and impressively stylish, Cielo is a relatively recent addition to Brum's restaurant scene and quickly became popular. The pal I took along to the review meal went back three times within a month!

The food is billed as Italian/Mediterranean which allows for a catch-all but appealing mix of risottos, pastas, charcuterie, calves' liver, fish etc.

It's pretty decent stuff with a rich squash, chorizo, chestnut and sage risotto and fried seabass with spinach both winning plaudits at a very favourable inspection meal.

City Cafe

Modern British

City Inn, Brindleyplace, Birmingham, B1 2HW.
www.cityinn.com
0121 643 1003.

Fresh, modern and good-looking - that's City Cafe, both in its decor and its food.

As is the rule with many of Birmingham's modern restaurants, it's a big place.

Lots of glass, strong lines, strong but very simple and understated, it is the very model of a modern restaurant interior.

The menu shows laudable ambition and innovation, with imaginative dishes that trawl the world for inspiration and are made special by competent cooking and quality of produce. Great care is taken over presentation and prices are sensible.

There's a good-value, stuff-yourself-silly Sunday lunchtime buffet too.

Coconut Lagoon

Indian

12 Bennetts Hill, Birmingham, B2 5RS.
www.coconutlagoon.com
0121 643 3045.

A très smart and colourful restaurant which offers something different from the run-of-the-mill Indian venues.

Coconut Lagoon specialises in the cuisine of southern India (unlike the familiar northern dishes) and trawls the states of Kerala, Goa, Karnataka and Andrha Pradesh for its tasty and carefully-spiced roster of dishes.

Fish, seafood, chicken, pork and lamb are all here, prepared with great care and served with pride and flair. Some may wish the portions were bigger but they were fine by me.

College of Food

Modern British

Summer Row, B3 1JB.
www.bcftcs.ac.uk
0121 604 1010.

The young catering students at this busy and highly-regarded college (it also teaches tourism and creative studies) get to try out their stuff in three eateries - the Atrium restaurant, the Brasserie and the Cap and Gown "pub".

Careful supervision is on hand at all times and the food is an absolute bargain - whether it's the grand fare of the Atrium restaurant with its French aspirations and comfy sofas, the no-nonsense bargain lunches of the Brasserie or the pub grub up on the seventh floor.

Times and hours follow term times and are so restricted that planning ahead is necessary, especially for the Atrium, which gets booked up months ahead.

Crowne Plaza Hotel

Modern British

NEC, Birmingham, B40 1PS.
www.birminghamnec.crowneplaza.com
0121 781 4000

Solid, satisfying dishes and interesting flavour combinations are on offer here.

Bare bistro-style tables, arty flowers and matey staff can't quite save it from the corporate hotel feel (it's too big for a start) but it's a pleasant enough place.

And unusually for the NEC complex, it has a decent view too - of the lake.

The food is robust and apart from some transglobal curiosities can lay serious claim to the ubiquitous "modern British" tag.

Del Villaggio

Italian

245 Broad Street, Birmingham, B1 2HL.
www.del-villaggio.com
0121 643 4224.

A stylish bar and eaterie concentrating on a plentiful choice of straightforward Italian fare which is generally good and competently cooked. Tables are a little squashed in, however, and the service can sometimes be brusque.

A sister establishment complete with deli is situated in the Bullring.

Good apple pies are a considerable part of our domestic happiness.

Jane Austen

Dial cafe bar

Pubs/bars

17 Thorp Street, Birmingham, B5 4U.
0121 622 5659.

A laidback and friendly place perfectly situated right next door to the Hippodrome Theatre for those in need of a pre- or post-theatre bite.

It's far more of a matey bar than a full-on restaurant experience which may or may not be what you're after.

It generally draws a younger crowd but the rustic interior with its stripped floors and bare tables is relaxed and the food keeps it pretty simple with such satisfying staples as potato skins, sausage and mash (with good Cumberland sausage of course), pastas and tuna steaks.

Service can be a bit ramshackle.

Digress

Pubs/bars

12-22 Edmund House, Newhall Street,
Birmingham, B3 3LX.
0121 200 0980.

The nearby offices provide the custom for this smart chrome and glass bar and restaurant in the commercial sector.

It's a big place (and there's a club next door) and though it seems to concentrate on drinks rather than food, it's actually a pretty good place to eat.

Early evening it can get packed with after-work revellers but it does calm down. The food is fuel on the hoof for the most part, with bruschetta and a snacks list including potato wedges, scampi and fries and chicken satay.

But the more serious stuff is surprisingly well done. A lamb shank was delightfully soft and tasty and a speedy salmon with coriander and roasted fennel and aubergines was a winner too. Little choice for veggies though.

This venue was for sale as we went to print.

Don Salvo

Italian

**156-158 Wharfside Street, the Mailbox,
Birmingham, B1 1RG.
0121 643 4000.**

The old Fish! site is now occupied by this smart and comfortable Italian restaurant, sister establishment of Geppettos in Wolverhampton.

In spite of the stylishly-modern decor, this is an Italian restaurant of the old school. Starters include half-melon filled wth port and main courses stack up bistecca and pollo in numerous guises.

There's lots of pasta too, as you'd expect, though only a couple of risottos. Fish specials are available daily though not listed on the menu.

It's generous, solidly hearty fare. Not River Cafe-style Italian, granted, but this style of food has legions of fans and hopefully they'll make the trip. It's a great waterside spot too.

Etcetera

Modern British

**42 High Street, Harborne,
Birmingham, B17 9NE.
www.etc-etera.co.uk
0121 428 2636**

The former California Pizza Factory has been revamped by its owners into a more grown-up, aspirational bar and restaurant.

The designerish new look works pretty well (though the low-lit restaurant verged on the gloomy).

The food shows welcome ambition, with the expected global pick 'n' mix range of dishes (pasta, risotto, steaks, tempura) enlivened by quirks of individuality.

Fonteyns

Modern British

17 Thorp Street, Birmingham, B5 4AT.
www.fonteyns.co.uk
0121 622 5757.

Ambitions are high at this swish bar and bistro whose name arose presumably from its close proximity to the Hippodrome's dance studios just across the street.

Perfectly placed, then, for the theatre and very impressive to look at too, all smart lilac and purple, and very comfortable.

The food keeps things simple with brasserie-style classics and the pretty upstairs room (formerly the main restaurant) is now available for private functions.

Goldies Brasserie at the Copthorne Hotel

Modern British

1 Paradise Circus, Birmingham, B3 3HJ.
www.copthornebirmingham.activehotels.com
0121 200 2727.

The Copthorne may look a little stranded in its sea of traffic (and facing an uncertain future with plans to demolish Paradise Circus altogether) but when it comes to location, location, location, it scores highly.

Although unavoidably hotelish in ambience, the food is surprisingly good and the service is eager to please.

Henry Wong

Chinese

283 High Street, Harborne, B17 9QH.
0121 427 7666.

A popular feature of well-heeled Harborne's restaurant scene for many years, Henry Wong has a chic interior, all smart black chairs and tablecloths, palms and metallic-effect mirrors.

There's more space than you'd expect behind the converted bank facade, with two connecting rooms and a small bar. But they manage to fill it all regularly thanks to a large menu that covers the expected territory reliably well. Service is friendly and efficient.

Hotel du Vin

Modern European

25 Church Street, Birmingham, B3 2NR.
www.hotelduvin.com
0121 236 0559.

A thoroughly French affair here with a romantic, candlelit restaurant at the heart of this utterly-chic hotel which made such magnificent use of the old eye hospital in the city's suits quarter.

There's no music, which may disappoint Charles Aznavour fans, but it's popular enough to have a constant background buzz of contented diners.

The menu covers all the basic French bistro bases with invention and a little fusion flair. Expect a lot of fish and a healthy Gallic respect for offal and bunny.

Service is eager to please and predominantly French and the wine list, naturally, is stupendous.

House of Fraser - Albert Roux restaurant

Modern British

Corporation Street, Birmingham, B2 5JS.
www.houseoffraser.co.uk
0121 236 8802.

Sometimes, a grabbed snack is no way to break up a day's serious shopping. Sometimes, you need a quiet, refined space to recharge or meet up with friends or colleagues.

The chic, contemporary surroundings of the Albert Roux restaurant provide a perfect escape. The entrance into this hidden haven is café-style with small, pale wood tables, but the restaurant proper is the full monty - rich blue walls and red, sumptuous yet modern seating.

These are rather formal yet comfortable surroundings and the menu offers the same sort of easy, classic style. Dishes change regularly but the warmer months, for instance, would typically see a wide range of salads predominating (we're in perfect ladies-who-lunch territory). Poached salmon, tuna and white bean and polenta with roast veg could be among the many options.

There may also be a gnocchi or pasta dish, perhaps a chicken fajita or tomato and mozzarella quesadilla.

Serious sandwiches are on offer too - and it's a great spot for afternoon tea with all the trimmings.

Next to eating good dinners, a healthy man with a benevolent turn of mind, must like, I think, to read about them.

WM Thackeray

Indi

Global

**Ladywell Walk, Arcadian Centre,
Hurst Street, B5 4ST.
0121 622 4858.**

Indian tapas is the idea here and a futuristic interior has been designed to match it.

The feeling of space is utilised to the full, while furniture is kept to a minimum. Walls are sparkling white and dining is on refectory-style long tables and bench seating.

The food is not just based on the Indian sub-continent and Spain but runs the gamut of Asian (including Chinese and Japanese) and Mediterranean flavours (Italian ones especially welcome).

Itihaas

Indian/global

**Islington Gates, Fleet Street,
Birmingham, B3 1JH.
www.itihaas.co.uk
0121 212 3383.**

An awful lot of money has been put into this big place on the corner of Newhall Street which straddles the business and jewellery quarters.

The decor is opulent, if a little odd in places with chandeliers lining one half of the dining room and a collection of lanterns on the other.

But the food is very good and obviously freshly made, with more unusual dishes that come not just from India but also from Kenya and there are Chinese influences here and there too.

Jam House

Pubs/bars

3-5 St Paul's Square, Hockley, B3 1QU.
www.thejamhouse.com
0121 200 3030.

Live music comes first here - and not surprisingly, in this Jools Holland-backed venture - but the food isn't too far behind.

It's a great fun venue. Seating on several levels allows for plenty of tables as well as room for standing and/or bopping.

You might be feeling too old for a nightclub (this is a sentiment that strikes women of a certain age but strangely, not their male contemporaries) but you can always come here when you want to let your hair down. It has exactly the right atmosphere of easy friendliness.

The menu offers world food to go with the world music. It aims high and is hearty, satisfying stuff.

Jessica's ★★

Modern French

1 Montague Road, Edgbaston,
Birmingham, B16 9HN
www.jessicasrestaurant.co.uk
0121 455 0999.

It was only a matter of time before Jessica's picked up a Michelin star - and sure enough, in 2005, it managed it, along with nearby Simpsons.

It's a slick operation in stylish, contemporary surroundings. Impressive enough for a special occasion yet friendly enough for a weekly visit.

The food may best be described as modern French. It bears many distinguished hallmarks from chef's Glynn Purnell's stint as deputy to Claude Bosi of Ludow's Hibiscus but it also has evidence of his years at the impressive Michelin-starred Simpsons in Kenilworth.

Glynn's a talented guy and this is a well-run place. A must-visit venue.

Jonathans

Modern British

**16 Wolverhampton Road, Oldbury,
West Midlands, B68 0LH.
www.jonathanshotel.activehotels.com
0121 429 3757.**

Jonathans has spread over the years into a veritable warren of dining areas and chintzy hotel bits.

The Victorian restaurant is something of a local institution with its intensely-laden decor.

It's all quite camp but the menu's aspirations are serious enough to give the plastic a good run for its money.

Jyoti

Indian/vegetarian

**569-571 Stratford Road, Sparkhill, B11 4LS.
0121 766 7199**

Vegetarian restaurants are rather thin on the ground these days but an Indian veggie restaurant has even more rarity value.

Its appeal, though, now that meat-eaters don't run screaming at the thought of a non-flesh-based meal, is pretty widespread. Yes, you can bring carnivores along here and they really won't be able to complain about lack of choice or flavour.

With 22 starters and 65 main courses, this is a vegetarian heaven. The food is amazingly cheap and it's unlicensed too, which makes it even more of a bargain.

Karibunis

Modern British

**South Birmingham College, Stratford Road/
Colebank Road, Hall Green, B28 8ES.**
www.sbirm.ac.uk
0121 694 5069.

If you're on the hunt for cheap food, forget the fast food
joint and try Karibunis.

This is the restaurant arm of the chefs' training centre
at South Birmingham College, which encourages keen
amateurs with evening courses as well as setting would-be
chefs on their way with GNVQs.

Forget any ideas of stylish surroundings and be forgiving
when faced with nervous young staff. But tuck into one of
the city's best bargains and enjoy it.

La Tasca

Spanish

**Regency Wharf, Broad Street,
Birmingham, B1 2DS.**
www.latasca.co.uk
0121 643 9888.

It may be a chain but La Tasca manages more than
adequately when it comes to offering fuel for the hungry
masses.

The tapas list is long and tempting and there are paellas
and tasty side orders to bewilder the indecisive. The slow-
cooked lamb (cordero en salsa) is especially good.

This is a big but warm and welcoming place and with its
dark wood, colourful tiles and mega chandeliers it all feels
good too, though service can be slipshod.

Las Iguanas

Latin American

Arcadian Centre, Hurst Street, B5 4TB.
www.iguanas.co.uk
0121 622 4466.

OK, so you don't come here for a sophisticated culinary blowout but you could do far worse when you just want a relaxed good time, perhaps with the children on a weekend lunchtime when the mood is particularly laidback (like the great salsa background music).

The food is standard Tex Mex, it's filling enough, it won't break the bank, the service is young and friendly and the refried beans aren't anything like as bad as they sound.

Lasan ★

Indian

Dakota Buildings, James Street,
Hockley, B3 1SD.
www.lasan.co.uk
0121 212 3664.

Forget any preconceptions of Indian restaurants. Lasan breaks the mould by providing not just a stunningly modern environment but also stunningly modern food.

Dishes are innovative, deft and delicious. Indian food goes haute cuisine. This is one of my favourite restaurants in Birmingham. Do try it.

Liaison

Modern British

**1558 Stratford Road, Hall Green,
Birmingham, B28 9HA**
www.liaisonrestaurant.co.uk
0121 733 7336

When you want a proper 'grown-up' restaurant, Liaison might well be the place for you.

Formally smart, it is the new creation of a couple whose original Liaison in Stratford-upon-Avon was a great hit a few years back. They've since been in Ireland but have decided to return and make Hall Green the surprising site of their latest venture.

Liaison offers self-consciously rather grand food, ornately presented and very labour intensive. One superb starter of black and white pudding with risotto involved chopping up the black pudding and reconstructing it with chunks of white pudding within it. The risotto was contained within a collar of filo pastry.

A lot of thought and care has gone into this food so you wouldn't expect it to be cheap but it's no rip-off either. Quite a special occasion place.

Living Room

Pubs/bars

**Regency Wharf, Broad Street,
Birmingham, B1 2DS.**
www.thelivingroom.co.uk
0121 616 6820.

The nice thing about the Living Room is that it feels slightly hidden away and secret. All you see from the street is a discreet ground floor lobby. There, a receptionist directs you into a lift and wow, like discovering Narnia through the back of a wardrobe, out you pop at the top into a smart piano bar.

Live music matters here in this comfortable, colonial-style room where ceiling fans whirr over the grand piano and wooden venetian blinds put stripes across the view.

The food, though, was a little mixed during the most recent inspection meal.

Locanta Piccalilli

Italian

31 Ludgate Hill, Hockley,
Birmingham, B3 1EH.
www.locanta.com
0121 236 7227.

This area of Hockley is stylish, genteel and up-and-coming so it's no surprise that new restaurants seem to be a regular event here.

Locanta Piccalilli is an Italian-based joint just off St Paul's Square, with a chef whose CV includes Pasta di Piazza and San Carlo.

It's in a good spot, looks the part and obviously wants to do well, with a menu that aims to please everyone, featuring pizzas, pastas and Italian fare alongside a magpie selection from other cultures.

Things were a bit hit and miss on the review visit but it was a friendly place which aims to please - and it was very new.

Mackenzie's

Modern British

5 The Citadel, Corporation Street, B4 6QD.
www.mackenziesbaranddiningroom.com
0121 236 4009.

A welcome arrival on the city scene, Mackenzie's aims high and makes some big claims but it is actually just as good as it says.

It occupies the old Quo Vadis site in the city's courts quarter but has transformed it with a new light and airy look - all very upmarket and stylish but relaxed with it.

The eating area takes precedence over the 'bar' side, which seems negligible, but the priorities are well-grounded as the food is very good - straightforward, modern good quality.

As we went to press, the future of Mackenzie's was uncertain but it was still operating.

Maharaja

Indian

23-25 Hurst Street, Birmingham, B5 4AS.
0121 622 2641.

The Maharaja prides itself very much on its quality reputation and serves up a favourite roll call of north Indian dishes to a fond and regular clientele.

The surroundings are traditional, the staff attentive and knowledgeable.

Classics, such as lamb rogan josh, are routinely praised for their restraint on the chilli while piling on rich flavours.

Malabar

Indian

103-105 High Street, Harborne, B17 9NR.
0121 428 4466/428 4499.

A little gem for one of Birmingham's well-to-do suburbs, Malabar is a "contemporary" Indian restaurant but it has the sense to keep all its options covered when it comes to the traditional stuff too.

So in nicely modern surroundings, it sets out its stall - an appealing mix of authenticity and aspiration - very attractively indeed.

The food is great, with a palpable feeling of effort and quality. But the best thing - and here I think they must be doing battle with their unlicensed Indian competitors - is a wine list which shows scarcely any mark-up at all. There's no need to bring your own with prices as low as these.

Malmaison ★

Modern British

The Mailbox, Birmingham, B1 1RF.
www.malmaison.com
0121 246 5000.

One of the most impressive places in the Mailbox, the Malmaison Hotel simply oozes style and quality.

Everything looks the part too. The bar is fantastic and the brasserie is just the last word in gorgeousness. Even the background music is great. The more sensitive amongst you may weep.

The menu doesn't put a foot wrong either with dishes that balance upmarket ingredients with comfort value. Whether it's risotto with pumpkin and sage, great burgers, good veggie options, this food succeeds because it links seasonality with quality and keeps it simple.

Comforting yet stylish too. An unbeatable combination.

Metro Bar and Grill ★

Pubs/bars

73 Cornwall Street, Birmingham, B3 2DF.
www.metrobarandgrill.co.uk
0121 200 1911.

Shiny, sleek and modern, the Metro bar is slap bang in the middle of Birmingham's suits quarter and a regular haunt for Birmingham's professional and commercial classes.

Its popularity is long-lived and understandable. With its quality food (it has a Michelin Bib Gourmand) and vibrant, lively atmosphere, the Metro feels like the place to be.

It's busy most of the time with a menu that gets an overhaul every four months. The dishes suggest a riot of flavours but the balancing act is a precision one with few things out of kilter. Simple tastes but well-blended, it makes for lively eating.

Michelle's La Bastille

French

20 Corporation Street, Birmingham, B4 6QB.
www.labastille.co.uk
0121 236 1171.

A genuine French feel pervades this big place up by the city's law courts.

Walk through the small bar at the front and discover a surprisingly large dining room lurking Tardis-like at the back.

Dark bentwood and mirrors dominate the place and a strongly Gallic menu offers lots of bargains, especially in the fixed price menus. Serviceable, unpretentious food for the cost-conscious.

Milano

Italian

The Arcadian Centre, Birmingham, B5 4ST.
www.milanorestaurant.co.uk
0121 622 3999.

A comfortable and friendly Italian which offers a great deal of quality throughout its big menu.

Excellent bruschetta, pasta and risottos, alongside a rack of bistecca, veak and pollo options provide both masses of comfort appeal and tons of fresh, well-cooked flavours.

No-nonsense, good food in a characterful environment.

Mix at Mechu ★

Modern British

45 Summer Row, Birmingham, B3 1JJ.
www.summerrow.com
0121 710 4222.

Set in one of Birmingham's more recent developments, Mix at Mechu aims at a more mature crowd than your typical Broad Street reveller.

They seem to enjoy it too. The smart crowd in their 20s and 30s flock here after work and at weekends to enjoy the stylish setting.

The bar (complete with mirror ball) is popular but the restaurant has lots to offer too, with masses of fish and seafood lined up alongside a list of tasty, well-executed favourites. Generous and eager to please.

Mokhams

Kashmiri

140 Digbeth, Birmingham, B5 6DR.
0121 643 7375.

The location isn't great - although Digbeth will improve dramatically with all the development work going on - but little Mokhams is still worth the trip.

This Kashmiri balti has nice touches which set it above the average. Indeed, its quality is its main claim to fame.

It's friendly, unassuming and cheap. It's also bring your own, so you can save even more.

Mongolian Bar

Mongolian

24 Ludgate Hill, Hockley, B3 1DX.
0121 236 3842.

A happy, relaxed, party place where you can collect ingredients as you go and hand them over to be cooked for you.

Follow the recipes they suggest or, if you're feeling creative, make up your own as you go along.

Opus ★

Modern British

54 Cornwall Street, Birmingham, B3 2DE.
www.opusrestaurant.co.uk
0121 200 2323.

An excellent, top quality new venture for the city from the team who once led Bank.

Opus is a chic yet unfussy place with acres of space and an army of friendly staff. A crustacea bar, with ranks of fresh shellfish, is a crowd-pleaser but there's more on offer than just that.

The food is spot-on - direct, robust flavours using premium ingredients and cooked by people who know what they're doing.

Everything at a review meal - from gazpacho to risotto to fish and chips - was perfect. Excellent wines too, with 30 available by the glass.

A crust eaten in peace is better than a banquet partaken in anxiety.

Aesop

Paris ★

Modern European

**109-111 Wharfside Street, The Mailbox,
Birmingham. B11RD.**
www.restaurantparis.co.uk
0121 632 1488

Paris is a haven of contemporary fine design and superb modern flavours tucked away in that temple to the designer label, the Mailbox.

While some may have grumbles about the high prices (a starter of scallops at £16, for example), most lavish praise on the slick set-up and exquisite food.

One of the city's premier restaurants.

Peppers

Indian

**Bishopsgate Street, off Broad Street,
Birmingham, B15 1AY.**
www.peppers-uk.co.uk
0121 633 4411.

Contemporary surroundings (including an amazing Michelangelo-style mural on the ceiling) form a smart backdrop to some decent Indian cooking here.

There are the expected inclusions but also some innovative twists. Nihari fishcakes, shahi machike kure (smoked salmon stuffed with peppered king prawns), battered spicy mushroom toped with paneer and peas... even lamb chops.

There's a lot of care being taken and it's an enjoyable stop-off before or after a trip to the UGC cinema next door. It's also a lot better than the food on offer from the neighbouring chains too.

Le Petit Blanc

French

2-3 Oozells Square, 9 Brindleyplace, B1 2HS.
www.blanc.co.uk
0121 633 7333.

Birmingham's Le Petit Blanc wowed the crowds when it opened its beautiful doors in 1999 and in July 2005 gave itself a facelift with a £400,000 refurb which saw it ditch the blue shades in favour of warm yellow walls and lots of brown leather seating.

The menu offers plenty of choice and prices are reasonable for such well-crafted yet simple dishes of reliable quality.

It's also a good place to take children - here they are warmly welcomed rather than tolerated and their menu doesn't have a chicken nugget in sight, hurrah.

It now faces a lot more competition and things have changed somewhat ownershipwise - with Raymond Blanc now owning just 25 per cent of the mini-chain and Loch Fyne the rest.

Poppyred

Pubs/bars

Arcadian Centre, Hurst Street,
Birmingham, B5 4TD.
www.poppy-red.com
0121 687 1200.

A smart and thriving trendy bar in the bustling (at night at least) clubs quarter.

Poppyred can get loud with music and crowds in the evening but also offers generally solid and well-priced fodder to keep its young clientele going.

Look out for bargain lunch deals. Tables outside available.

Prana Restaurant and Lounge ★

Modern British

121 Suffolk Street, Birmingham, B1 1LX.
www.pranarestaurant.co.uk
0121 616 2211.

Prana is a mega-stylish haunt right next door to the Mailbox and perfectly placed for the Alexandra and Hippodrome theatres.

The feel, with its dramatic red and black decor and low lighting, is swanky nightclub but it is distinctly aspirational when it comes to the food served at its many tables.

Whether it's Sevruga caviar followed by grilled lobster knocked back with a glass of one of the many champagnes on offer, this is certainly a place where you can push the boat out when needed but there's also lots of more comforting (though equally high quality) fare on offer, from pork belly pot roast to homemade Cumberland sausage and mash.

Prana is a restaurant the city can rightly feel proud of.

Primitivo

Pubs/bars

10-12 Barwick Street, city centre, B3 2NT.
0121 236 6866.

Deep in Birmingham's commercial sector, Primitivo cuts its cloth to fit its professional and predominantly male clientele, not just with an arty interior and bijou trendy bar but with easy-eating food that is reliably good quality.

It's friendly, of course, and lunchtimes and after-work find the place doing exceptionally well. Food is mainly Mediterranean-based with reasonable pasta dishes, good fish and competently-cooked meat.

Rajdoot Tandoori

Indian

78-79 George Street, Hockley, B3 1PY.
www.rajdoot.co.uk
0121 643 8805.

Rajdoot claims a place not just in Birmingham's restaurant heritage but the country's - it is said that they were the first to introduce tandoori cooking into the UK back in 1966.

There are now sibling Rajdoots in Manchester, Bristol and Dublin but the Brum granddaddy, now rehomed in up-and-coming Hockley, keeps its head held high.

In the large, traditional ornate interior, the tandoor specialities are as popular as ever but fish Amritsari (spicily-battered cod in a garlicky tomato sauce) and lamb Punjabi are also regulars in a lengthy list of favourites.

Red Peppers

Modern European

117 Wharfside Street, the Mailbox, B1 1RF.
0121 643 4202.

A feelgood and family-friendly yet smart place which occupies the spot once home to Ink in the well-to-do Mailbox centre.

There are no airs and graces here - indeed, the catch-all menu is so eager to please, it offers everything from pizza and pasta to bouillabaisse and moussaka.

There's even hefty stuff too like tagine-style lamb shank and gorgonzola steak.

Despite the amount of choice, standards are decent and everything hits the spot, whether it's a tasty red pepper hummus starter or a satisfying, glazed pork belly main course.

The young service is efficient and the crowds already seem to have taken it to their hearts. Sensible prices defy the designer-label location.

Ruby Cantonese

Chinese

Barnsley Road, Edgbaston, B17 8ED.
0121 429 8805.

A solidly good neighbourhood Chinese restaurant, Ruby is also friendlier than many and well deserves its loyal local following.

The warm, brightly-lit room has a huge, red pan-tiled pretend pagoda roof along one wall and an army of bustling staff.

A view of the kitchen also allows sightings of the many chefs needed to cope with the heavyweight volume which is the menu.

Quality is mostly good, though inevitably perhaps, some dishes score more highly than others.

Saint Pauls

Pubs/bars

50-54 St Paul's Square, Hockley,
Birmingham, B3 1QS.
0121 605 1001.

The look is archetypal wine bar - stripped floors and tables, bare brick, some lively colours here and there - and it's been a winner for Saint Paul's for years now.

Brunch has now been added to their rota of meal times. Otherwise, it's lunch and dinners as usual with a tempting list of bistro stuff. It mostly hits the mark and pricing is sensible.

It's a small place but it feels good. When the going gets tough and busy, the hungry get downstairs or perhaps even to an outside table if the weather's OK. After-work drinkers from nearby offices love it.

Santa Fe

American/Mexican

**178-180 Wharfside Street, the Mailbox,
Birmingham, B1 1RN.
www.santafe.co.uk
0121 632 1250.**

Santa Fe has a great waterside view but its interior - which announces its south-west US roots in style - is looking a little tired round the edges these days.

But it's still equally good for a pals' night out, a pig-out à deux or a family weekend treat. Happily, the food is a world apart from ubiquitous chain Tex Mex fodder (although Santa Fe is itself part of a mini-chain and the culinary work of chef Rocky Durham).

The Mexican feel is there - quesadillas, chillies, tortilla chips, salsa and guacamole abound - but it's done very well.

Selfridges ★

Global

**The Bullring, Birmingham, B5 4BP.
www.selfridges.com
08708 377377.**

Selfridges - the store that was beamed in from outer space and rejuvenated Birmingham's image overnight - is a haven for the hungry shopper.

Its cool, funky food hall packs in more delights per square inch than a gourmet Tardis. A wide variety of eating areas provide food for every mood, whether it's delicious noodles, seafood, fab Italian, brasserie favourites, sushi or just a coffee and fragrant pastry. Simply park yourself on a bar stool and tuck in. The quality is as high as you'd expect and service is snappy.

The excellent food counters are to drool over too. Cheeses, charcuterie, breads, all sorts of ready-prepared meat joints and fish are all exceptional, both for variety and flavour.

The Gallery Restaurant upstairs is also a winner.

Shimla Pinks

Indian

214 Broad Street, Birmingham, B15 1AY.
www.shimlapinks.com
0121 633 0366.

The Indian restaurant that broke the flocked-wallpaper mould, Shimlas is still going strong several years down the line with a mid-Broad Street spot that may have seemed a little out of the way at one time but now looks positively inspired.

The place these days sports a cool, 60s retro look, with swirly lights and hints of Austin Powers. A line of ghostly mannequins guards the entrance and the cavernous space is divided up into lots of smaller seating areas.

When it gets busy - which is often the case - it can get very loud.

Shogun Sushi and Noodle Bar

Japanese

113-115 Wharfside Street, the Mailbox,
Birmingham, B1 1RF.
www.shogunteppanyaki.com
0121 623 1253.

Cool, minimalist and serene, the Mailbox Shogun is a temple to icy oriental style.

A good variety of sushi and sashimi is available - either at the famous conveyor belt or at the teppan-yaki tables.

Although fish is the star of the show, the menu also offers lots of choice away from the sea too, including meat dishes and vegetable tempura.

But this is a fish-eater's heaven, with king prawns with garlic and plum wine and salmon with butter and soya sauce both particular favourites.

Shogun Teppenyaki

Japanese

The Water's Edge, Brindleyplace,
Birmingham, B1 2HL.
www.shogunteppanyaki.com
0121 643 1856.

Food is theatre in this cool black and white Japanese eaterie with the chefs taking centre stage amid a mountain of fish and cleavers, their arena the huge steel hotplate where they cook the food in front of your table.

It's not cheap but it can be a fun place for groups who fancy culinary cabaret.

Sibila's at Body and Being

Vegetarian

The Watermarque, 100 Browning Street,
Birmingham, B16 8EH.
www.sibilasrestaurant.co.uk
0121 456 7633.

In a superb canalside location, the airy café-style restaurant of this chic spa serves up good, fresh, vegetarian food for the Noughties.

Take a seat by the light-filled windows and watch the boats go by as you tuck into such fare as mushroom and chestnut pate, baked chicory with cannellini bean cream and parmesan or one of the pastas or salads.

It's all decent quality and organic with many drinks also carrying the Fair Trade marque. A relaxed and friendly place.

The spa itself specialises in holistic, anti-stress treatments and also offers yoga, pilates and tai chi classes.

Simpsons ★★

Modern British

20 Highfield Road, Edgbaston, Birmingham.
www.simpsonsrestaurant.co.uk
0121 454 3434.

There is simply nothing like Simpsons in Birmingham.

This superbly-refurbished grade two listed building in leafy Edgbaston has one of the city's premier restaurants, offering superb food which has rightly won it a Michelin star.

But there's even more to it than that. There are four sumptuous bedrooms, a cookery school and a private dining room too.

The restaurant is in the orangery which has now been glassed in and given a very upmarket but thoroughly comfortable look.

It's not particularly expensive given the quality and standard of cooking skills. Definitely a must-visit venue.

Sobar

Oriental

Arcadian Centre, Hurst Street,
city centre, B5 4TD.
www.sobar.co.uk
0121 693 5084.

Birmingham's first noodles bar, Sobar is a trendy little joint, all low brown leather seats and minimalist wooden chairs in this odd little centre off Hurst Street.

Music matters and evenings get very loud. There's a DJ set-up in a corner and a small dance floor for those who feel able to move after fry-ups like Japanese-style tempura vegetables (probably carrot, courgette and onion) served with a nice, sweet, chilli sauce dip and chicken and shiitake mushrooms with pak choi and noodles in oyster sauce.

Tarnished Halo

Pubs/bars

**21 Ludgate Hill, Hockley,
Birmingham, B3 1DW.
www.tarnished-halo.co.uk
0121 236 7562.**

Here is yet another bar/restaurant aimed at the office/
arty/stylish crowd which makes you wonder just how
many restaurants little Hockley can take.

It's decent quality though, if a little short on the wow
factor. Expect the modern standard bistro dishes served
with a friendly smile in a relaxed, modern environment.
Tables outside too on some smart decking.

Thai Edge

Thai

**7 Oozells Square, Brindleyplace,
Birmingham, B1 2HL.
www.thaiedge.co.uk
0121 643 3993.**

Some may carp about allegedly less than authentic aspects
to parts of the interior at this consummately stylish
restaurant but I guess the vast majority of the diners
are unlikely to get their tom yums in a twist over such
matters.

After all, it looks good and it tastes good and that's pretty
well all that's required for the most part.

Staff in opulent purple are wreathed in smiles and greet
everyone beautifully. The place looks fabulous, as does
the food.

Fish and seafood are the key players but there are plenty
of fascinating vegetable dishes either as side orders or
star attractions.

Thai Orchid

Thai

7 Bennetts Hill, Birmingham, B2 5ST.
www.thaigroup.com
0121 212 1000

One of a small chain, Thai Orchid's Birmingham branch is housed in a former bank down a sedate city centre side street.

Brightly-coloured floral plaques are interspersed among the old wooden panelling, oriental statues stand guard beneath the high windows and pots of trailing greenery dangle from the ceiling.

But it's the food that's pulling in the punters. Quality and variety is good - whether you're choosing from a lunchtime all-you-can-eat buffet or the a la carte.

Service is very friendly and it's good value. Well-placed too for business lunches.

Tin Tin

Chinese

The Water's Edge, Brindleyplace,
Birmingham, B1 2HL.
0121 633 0888.

A big Chinese restaurant with a seemingly-unabating popularity, Tin Tin's first floor situation gives it a fine vantage point over the Brindleyplace crowds, although the smallish circular windows don't provide too much of a view.

Luckily, the kitchen seems well able to cope with its hordes of fans, even if the waiting staff can seem overstretched and occasionally forgetful.

La Toque d'Or ★

French

27 Warstone Lane, Hockley,
Birmingham, B18 6JQ.
www.latoquedor.co.uk
0121 233 3655.

It was a sad day when Didier Philipot announced he was going to sell his Toque d'Or restaurant in Hockley for it is that rare thing in Birmingham - a small, individually-owned restaurant with the owner slaving away in the kitchen.

Happily for us - although admittedly not so good for him - it still hadn't sold as we went to print so you may yet have a chance to get along there.

The food is deliciously unfussy yet classy. The quality is excellent and it's great value for money. Don't expect massive servings (and especially not of veg) - this is concentrated stuff to savour.

The restaurant is small but attractive and romantic (another rarity for the city), with bare brick walls and pretty stained glass windows.

Ty's Jazz and Spice

Kashmiri

132 Stratford Road, Sparkbrook, B11 1AJ.
www.tys-jazzspice.co.uk
0870 0660 069 (day) 0870 0660 868 (eve).

The first and only Kashmiri jazz bar and restaurant, Ty's is named after owner Ty Mamood and is an extraordinary place all round - a converted bank, grade 2 listed and looking rather stately in cream with a smart door canopy.

The interior is pretty cool too, with wooden blinds, high ceilings and stripped floor. The performers may be more King Pleasure and the Biscuit Boys than Miles Davis (call for details) but it makes for a fun, if very loud, evening.

The food is more expensive than your average Indian restaurant but takes account of the fact that often you're getting a band thrown in.

Valentino's

Italian

**73 High Street, Harborne,
Birmingham, B17 9NS.
www.valentinosrestaurant.net
0121 427 2560.**

An old stager on the Harborne scene, Valentinos seems to have been on the high street for ever.

It has many loyal fans too for its solid, reliable Italian fare. The old favourites are here in a longish menu added to by a specials board. Fish is plentiful, as is pasta and risottos.

Traditional in style and cuisine but that's just how its fans like it.

Wagamama

Japanese

**The Bullring, Birmingham, B5 4QL.
www.wagamama.com
0121 633 3033.**

The ever-expanding chain has finally made it into Brum with a busy and buzzy place in the Bullring.

It's not the most comfortable dining ever, with its utilitarian benches, but the food is good and obviously freshly made and the prices are very reasonable.

The only criticism - especially for groups eating together - is that the dishes can arrive at widely differing times. Be prepared to share...

> *An alcoholic is someone you don't like who drinks as much as you do.*
>
> *Dylan Thomas*

Warehouse Café

Vegetarian

**54-57 Allison Street, Digbeth,
Birmingham, B5 5TH.**
www.thewarehousecafe.com
0121 633 0261.

The trusty Warehouse café has been a part of Birmingham veggie life for ever and still maintains a faithful following prepared to seek it out in its hidden-away spot.

It's more than worth the stroll. Up in the pine-dominated first floor caff, the food is good quality and cheap and served with easy friendliness.

It's also a comfortable place to go and eat if you're solo. Some dishes are tried and tested regulars (cashew nut pate and houmous, for instance), or there may be tagines, curried dishes or a flan with a selection of tasty salads.

Unlicensed but with interesting soft drinks on offer for those who don't want to bring their own.

West 12

Modern British

**Marriott Hotel, Hagley Road, Five Ways,
Birmingham, B16 8SJ.**
www.marriotthotels.com
0121 452 1144.

The Marriott dumped its grand old Sir Edward Elgar restaurant and more informal Langtry's for this new urban-look eaterie.

Big banquettes (straight from a first class railway carriage for giants) and no tablecloths are the current style and the food, though good, can seem on the pricey side. It has a feel of quality - in the service certainly - but lacks a certain soul.

Wing Wah

Chinese

278 Thimble Mill Lane, Nechells, B7 5HD.
www.wingwah.net
0121 327 7879.

Wing Wah is part of the flamboyantly-oriental complex which also houses the Wing Yip supermarket and warehouse - a big and hugely successful bit of Chinatown not far from the city centre.

I hesitate to trot out the old adage about how it must be good because it's full of Chinese diners - after all, do the Chinese look at McDonald's and say it must be good because it's full of English people?

But the evidence here seems overwhelming; it's an enormous place, always busy and always, yes, with Chinese (it's so handy when you've done your shopping next door) but by no means totally so.

The turnover is so fast and furious that hot, fresh food can be relied upon. Service is brisk and there are as-much-as-you-can-eat buffets, although the food in these isn't in the same league as the a la carte.

Wongs ★

Chinese

5-11 Fleet Street, Birmingham, B3 1JP.
0121 212 1888.

It took 12 months of hard labour to turn this formerly-derelict site on the edge of the Jewellery Quarter (just round the corner from Mechu) into a smart - and pretty vast - restaurant.

But Henry Wong managed it and now has what must be the best Chinese restaurant in town. The food here is excellent - utterly fresh, brilliantly cooked and packed with well-balanced flavour, just as it should be.

The service is friendly and efficient and Wong's extras include a small Chinese-style courtyard if you fancy eating al fresco and a private dining room which can seat about 20.

XE - Xaymaca Experience

Jamaican

34 Bristol Street, Birmingham, B5 7AA.
www.xaymaca.co.uk
0121 622 3332.

Not many venues will suggest that you limbo from the bar into the restaurant but they do at Xaymaca. It is then, a bit of a party place, friendly, laidback, a little bit of Jamaica on the mean streets of Brum.

The menu offers a contemporary version of Caribbean cuisine but if traditional stuff is what you're after, it's certainly here, with goat curries and ackee and saltfish among the pepperpot soups, calaloo and plantain, cassava and yam.

Zagora

Moroccan

4 Fletchers Walk, Paradise Circus,
Birmingham.
www.zagorarestaurant.co.uk
0121 233 2484.

Zagora, being a Moroccan restaurant, is something of a rarity for Birmingham and it's rather a wacky place.

Sited in the draughty and depressing underpass Fletcher's Walk, it has a warmly over-the-top interior, all sofas and fancy wall decorations and even a hookah, but it still exudes homeliness.

The food - lots of lamb, couscous and tagines, as you'd expect - is basically OK and the service is friendly enough but far from slick. A little ramshackle but endearing.

Zinc Bar and Grill

Pubs/bars

**Regency Wharf, adjacent to Hyatt Hotel,
Birmingham, B1 2SD.**
www.conran.com
0121 200 0620. Fax 0121 200 0630.

Terence Conran's Birmingham presence is as cleverly designed as you'd expect, sparse and beautifully-lit. A hefty spiral staircase to the first floor is the star of the show.

This upstairs space is wonderful, a fabulous place to sit, with a terrace lining the frontage over the canal basin which beckons in warm weather. Once it was all dining room but the bar has proved more successful and drinkers have consequently taken over part of it.

The menu is straightforward, prices are on the high side but pretty much the going rate for the quality is there and service is friendly.

Starters may include Loch Fyne smoked salmon or caesar salad while mains fature hearty and homely stuff such as honey-roast pork belly with champ or steak and kidney pie.

It's all nicely unfaffy yet in a chic, urban setting.

Life is so brief that we should not glance either too far backwards or forwards... therefore study how to fix our happiness in our glass and in our plate.

Grimod de la Reynière

BISHOPS TACHBROOK

Mallory Court ★

Fine dining

**Harbury Lane, Bishops Tachbrook,
Leamington Spa, Warwickshire, CV33 9QB.
www.mallory.co.uk
01926 330214.**

As if it wasn't enough having a beautiful house in a beautiful place and with beautiful grounds, Mallory Court gets everything else right too.

It's not cheap of course, but the quality is excellent (it has a Michelin star thanks to head chef Simon Haigh) and the setting divine. They've also got some great staff who manage to create an aura of ease and comfort rather than stuffy formality - a real gift.

A lovely terrace is available for outdoor dining and hotel guests are in for many luxurious treats (the hotel is a member of the prestigious Relais et Chateaux group) - there's an outdoor swimming pool, as well as tennis courts and a croquet lawn.

A brasserie was due to open in September 2005.

BOURNHEATH

Nailers Arms

Pubs/bars

**62 Doctor's Hill, Bournheath,
Bromsgrove, B61 9JE.
www.thenailersarms.com
01527 873045.**

Bournheath is a dinky little village just outside the throbbing metropolis of Bromsgrove. It has more hostelries than it really deserves - two or three at least within staggering distance of each other - but the Nailer's Arms is the best destination for the starving.

This is a country pub with a staggeringly modern interior (think Habitat in the Woolpack), and is as splendidly ambitious in its food as its decor.

Dishes like Thai-spiced mussels, cumin-spiced salmon and fillet steak with herb polenta and wild mushrooms are designed to impress as well as satisfy and for the most part carry it off with some ease.

BRIMFIELD

The Roebuck

Pubs/bars

Brimfield, Ludlow. SY8 4NE.
www.theroebuckinn.com
01584 711230.

It seems rather greedy that Ludlow's gourmet reputation even extends to some of the village pubs in its outlying regions.

The Roebuck may be a rather inconspicuous inn but in the beamed, cosy interior of the three bars or the sunny, contemporary dining room, a knowledgeable menu offers modern brasserie standards like duck confit as well as traditional roasts and steamed steak and mushroom suet pudding.

Lygon Arms

Fine dining

High Street, Broadway, Worcs, WR12 7DU.
www.thelygonarms.co.uk
01386 852255.

Broadway is one of the must-see villages in the Cotswolds but has nowhere near as many good eating places as nearby Chipping Campden. What it has got, of course, is the world-famous Lygon Arms.

The Lygon has been renowned for hundreds of years as a coaching inn and is considered one of the Cotswolds' finest hotels. It appeals hugely to the American market as a typical slice of olde England.

Its top guy in the kitchen is outstanding chef Martin Blunos, who has brought it a Michelin star.

Russell's ★

Modern British

20 High Street, The Green, Broadway,
Worcestershire.
www.russellsofbroadway.co.uk
01386 853555.

In this beautiful Cotswolds village, a very chic and modern restaurant is housed within the ancient, honeyed walls of 20 High Street. It used to be the base of renowned furniture designer Gordon Russell, hence the name.

The co-owner of the new eaterie is Barry Hancox, who used to be manager of the nearby Lygon Arms.

Here, with partner Andrew Riley, he's created a lovely upmarket venue. Pricy, as you'd expect, but with seriously aspirational food using classy ingredients and interesting flavour combinations.

The execution was a mite patchy on an inspection visit but the overall impression was of one classy joint.

BROMSGROVE

Grafton Manor

Fine dining

Grafton Lane, Bromsgrove, Worcs, B61 7HA.
www.graftonmanorhotel.co.uk
01527 579007.

You have to fit in around wedding parties when you want to dine at Grafton Manor these days but it's still worth the effort.

The setting is impressive - a grand 16th century building (although largely rebuilt in the 18th century) with its own chapel and grounds, some of which are pressed into use producing herbs, fruit and veg for the hotel's kitchens.

The place is family-run and chef Simon Morris (son of the owner) is a renowned Indiaphile, whose eastern influences colour the menu and also lead to a feast of Indian cooking in the early part of each year. (He has also won various curry chef awards).

So, among the stolidly upper class English/French fare, expect to see, for example, some very good Bombay prawns, perhaps with a trio of sauces (all Empire-led) or some delicious Goan bread.

BUCKLAND

Buckland Manor

Fine dining

Buckland, near Broadway, Worcs. WR12 7LY.
www.bucklandmanor.co.uk
01386 852626.

Everyone will be on their best behaviour in this gorgeous little pearl of Cotswold fine dining.

Electric gates let you into the grounds, then it's along the tree-lined gravel drive up to the entrance.

It's serious, sophisticated fare but right on the button - fresh, simply-cooked fish, game when in season, the best beef - beautifully presented and executed.

Buckland is a Relais et Chateaux hotel so it has all the luxury paraphernalia you'd expect, croquet lawn and swimming pool included.

It can be intimidating but treat it with respect, your best clothes, five hours of your time (it should never be rushed) and a flexible wallet and you're in for a memorable occasion.

CANNOCK

Zafroni

Indian

4th and 5th floors, Virage Point, Virage Park, Walsall Road, Bridgtown, Cannock, WS11 3NH. www.zafroni.com 01543 505023.

A stunning view is the great bonus of Zafroni, a smartly-modern Indian restaurant which perches on the fourth and fifth floors in downtown Bridgtown. Not Manhattan admittedly but still impressive at night.

After a drink in the fourth floor bar, sashay upstairs and try out the lengthy menu.

All the usual favourites are there, along with some more unusual and "connoisseur" dishes. Salmon in a spicily-rich marinade of dill, fennel, ginger and mustard oil (machli tikka malika) made a tasty starter and a Durdesh main course speciality of kaddie korai ghosht - lamb braised with various spices - also won praise.

You may well find equally good curries cheaper but can they offer a comparable view?

CHADDESLEY CORBETT

Brockencote Hall Hotel ★

Fine dining

Chaddesley Corbett, Kidderminster, Worcs. DY10 4PY.
www.brockencotehall.com
01562 777876.

Jerome Barbancon is the French chef here, providing elegant, impressive food for a well-heeled clientele.

The village of Chaddesley Corbett is delightful and Brockencote, despite its typically English surroundings, looks just like a French chateau. It sits regally in 70 acres of lovely Worcestershire greenness, the grounds dotted with sheep.

A dramatically-large conservatory sits next to the south-facing dining rooms; all are chintzily formal but very comfortable - a fitting background for the formal yet delicious fare on offer.

CHADWICK END

The Orange Tree

Pubs/bars

Warwick Road, Chadwick End, Warwickshire, B93 0BN.
www.orangetreepub.co.uk
01564 785364.

It's Warwickshire, it's gorgeously trendy, the menu has "eat me" written all over it and the staff are young and beautiful... it could only be another Paul Salisbury/Paul Hales pub.

It's the perfect setting for a stylishly-direct menu which offers food that's young and fun, simple but impressive. Pizzas and pastas are all there as well as salads, duck confit, spit gammon and crushed potato, steaks and calves' liver. Not just any old chips here either but- Belgium fries which come with mayo, continental style.

Le Champignon Sauvage★★

Modern Europe

**24-26 Suffolk Road, Cheltenham,
Glos, GL50 2AQ.
www.lechampignonsauvage.co.uk
01242 573449.**

Startling things go on in this bright yet homely restaurant, which boasts two Michelin stars (what an achievement - there are only nine others in the country).

With chef-patron David Everitt-Matthias at the helm (and at the very top of his game), the cooking displays a rare degree of concentrated effort and impressive skill from a strongly-French base.

Coupled with a culinary imagination which fires on all cylinders, it makes for the sort of menu that foodies dream about - highly complex yet perfectly harmonious.
A meal here will linger in your memory.

Le Petit Blanc

French

**The Promenade, Cheltenham, Glos, GL50 INN.
www.blanc.com
01242 266800.**

Within the regal splendour of the pristine Queens Hotel, Le Petit Blanc brasserie offers a look that is consummately stylish, with an arty food mural fencing in a spacious room filled with shiny metallic tables and divided from the kitchen by swish opaque glass doors.

As mentioned on the entry for Le Petit Blanc, Birmingham, there have been some changes at the top and Raymond Blanc's stake is now 25 per cent.

Cotswold House Hotel - Garden Room restaurant ★

Fine dining

The Square, Chipping Campden, Glos, GL55 6AN.
www.cotswoldhouse.com
01386 840330.

The beautiful Cotswold House Hotel offers two exceptional restaurants - the formal, exquisite Garden Room and the buzzy, contemporary brasserie Hicks.

You can't go wrong with either - it just depends on what mood you're in. In both places, you'll get superb food.

In Hicks, the emphasis is on informal, satisfying fare with bags of round-the-world flavours.

In the Garden Room, you're in the special occasion world of amuse-bouches and showstopping, formal but fabulous dishes.

It's a glorious restaurant, with lovely French windows looking out over a pretty terrace. Service is helpful rather than overbearing and the food is a revelation.

Cotswold House Hotel - Hicks brasserie ★

Modern British

The Square, Chipping Campden, Glos, GL55 6AN.
www.cotswoldhouse.com
01386 840330.

Hicks' brasserie is a surprisingly urban and chic eaterie within the Cotswold House Hotel in gorgeous Chipping Campden.

While its sibling restaurant the Garden Room offers special occasion cuisine and a more formal (yet unstuffy) air,

Hicks is a buzzy place with a youthful and contemporary feel - and food to match.

This is relaxed, everyday eating out the way we all want it today. The surroundings feel good and the menu offers delicious, eclectic fare that won't break the bank, whether you're just after a great steak and chips or a delicious risotto. Great vegetarian choice too.

Eight Bells Inn

Pubs/bars

Church Street, Chipping Campden,
Glos, GL55 6JG.
01386 841669.

Tucked away down one of this lovely village's many lovely streets, this 14th century building really looks the part: little mullioned windows, warm stone walls, flagstoned floors, beams - the works.

The food is decent and there's a small garden too.

Noel Arms Hotel ★

Oriental/European

High Street, Chipping Campden,
Gloucestershire, GL56 6AT.
www.noelarmshotel.com
01386 840317.

Strangely, this traditional hotel with its pubby bar now offers great Oriental (especially Thai) food - though there is also a briefer 'European' selection for those in the bar if they're not in the mood.

It seems to be doing great business and the food is excellent - vibrantly fresh and packed with balanced and zingy flavours. A great wake-up call for your tastebuds.

The place is owned by the couple who have the Cotswold House Hotel opposite, where standards are equally high. (See separate entries opposite for the hotel and its Hicks brasserie.)

CLENT

Bell and Cross ★

Pubs/bars

Holy Cross, Clent, Worcs, DY9 9QL.
www.bellandcrossclent.co.uk
01562 730319.

This listed building nestling at the foot of the Clent Hills has one huge advantage in the world of pub grub - it is run by top chef Roger Narbett, who is in charge of this highly-successful venture with capable wife Jo. (They also have the Chequers at Cutnall Green near Droitwich).

The emphasis is on modern, satisfying fare that wouldn't be out of place in a swish little bistro - from grilled Scottish rib-eye steak with chips to Cornish seafood fishcakes with prawns to farmhouse terrines.

The pubby look has been carefully preserved, with the various little rooms still intact, having escaped the late 20th century developers' hatchet job that ruined so many traditional inns.

There is also a sizeable garden with plenty of tables for drinking and dining al fresco. It's always busy and booking is always advisable.

Fountain Inn

Pubs/bars

Adams Hill, Clent, Worcs, DY9 9PU.
01562 883286.

Clent is rural enough and yet within easy reach of Birmingham for the Fountain to do more than averagely well out of visiting Brummies who fancy a night, or a lunch, in the country.

The food is generally sturdy pub grub, with some dishes more successful than others.

The legend in its own lunch and dinner time is the lamb pot roast, an enormous great plateful of meat cooked long and slow till it almost falls off the bone.

COLWALL

Colwall Park Hotel ★

Fine dining

Walwyn Road, Colwall, Malvern, WR13 6QG.
www.colwall.com
01684 540000

Colwall Park is a special venue. The backdrop - genteel, Daily Telegraph country hotel - is rather staid and the service is decidedly unhurried but it's all worth it for the fine fare.

Quality counts here in the stylish, contemporary dining room, whether it's an excellent 'pressing of marinated vegetables', delicious crispy wild seabass or superb 'assiette of Ryeland lamb'.

The journey is stunningly scenic too. This is a lovely part of the world and even if your journey home is in the dark, there are pretty light-strewn vistas to feast your eyes upon.

As well as the no-smoking Seasons restaurant, the hotel also has the Lantern Bar offering light meals and snacks.

CORSE LAWN

Corse Lawn House Hotel ★

Fine dining

Corse Lawn, near Tewkesbury,
Gloucestershire. GL19 4LZ.
www.corselawnhousehotel.co.uk
01452 780771.

A dream of a place situated out in gorgeous countryside near Tewkesbury, this exquisite, listed Queen Anne house is run by the Hine family of Cognac fame.

Corporate it ain't. There is real personality in evidence here, from the hearty, front-of-house style to the tantalising menu masterminded by Baba Hine in the kitchen.

The impressive kitchen skills have no airs and graces but an impeccable sense of taste. A perfect spot for a drive out on a sunny Sunday.

COVENTRY

The Gallery restaurant

Modern British

**20 Earlsdon Street, Earlsdon,
Coventry, CV5 6EG.
www.thegalleryrestaurant.co.uk
02476 13222.**

A modern restaurant with a long menu packed with contemporary flavours and bursting with ingredients.

It's friendly enough and the food is fine but at weekends the noisy bar downstairs is offputting - especially if you're after a quiet meal out.

CROWLE GREEN

Old Chequers

Pubs/bars

**Crowle Green, near Crowle,
near Worcester, WR7 4AA.
01905 381275.**

If übertrendy gastro pubs aren't your style, you'll feel much more at home at the Old Chequers in this cute village near Worcester.

But although the decor - olde beams and pubby dark wood tables - may be traditional, the food offers a mega blackboard of choice and keeps its regular army of faithfuls very happy indeed.

CUTNALL GREEN

Chequers ★

Pubs/bars

**Kidderminster Road, Cutnall Green,
near Droitwich, Worcestershire, WR9 0PJ.
www.chequerscutnallgreen.co.uk
01299 851292.**

Not content with keeping foodies over Clent way happy with the wonderful Bell and Cross, Jo and Roger Narbett now enjoy even more success with their second country pub venture about 20 minutes away - the Chequers, in a pretty village near Droitwich.

This is a much bigger concern and also a lot bolder as far as the decor goes, with zippily-vibrant colours between the venerable pale beams.

It looks great, a perfect mix of trendy and olde, and offers masses of space as well as truly excellent food.

DAYLESFORD

Daylesford Organic farmshop café ★

Modern British

**Daylesford, near Kingham, Glos, GL56 0YG.
01608 731700.**

A farmshop the like of which you've never seen before with a cafe which is the last word in Sunday supplement style.

Top-to-toe gorgeousness is the byword here, with much of the wonderful produce being created or grown here, from artisan cheeses and breads to fab fruit and veg - and all of it organic.

The cafe offers a small but perfectly formed selection of light lunch dishes using their own ingredients, naturally. Simple but quality stuff such as soups, dips, courgette flowers filled with chicken mousse, quiches... chi chi to an almost ethereal level.

DICKENS HEATH

Mortons Kitchen, Bar and Deli ★

Modern British

Market Square, Dickens Heath, nr Solihull, B90 1UB. www.mortonskitchen.co.uk 0121 744 2884.

The rather odd new village of Dickens Heath has a huge bonus in this super trendy and funky place from Mssrs Pauls Salisbury and Hales.

It's a buzzy, big space, colourful and friendly, with simple, robust and deeply appealing food.

The deli is neatly tucked away in the corner, while the rest of the space is given over to casual, yet good quality, eating and drinking.

It's young, fun and a great place to hang out. Great for Sunday brunch too.

DORRIDGE

Forest Hotel ★

Modern British

Station Approach, Dorridge, Solihull, B93 8JA.
www.forest-hotel.com

This smartly-refurbished hotel (owned by the same couple who have Etcetera in Harborne, Birmingham) has a chic, contemporary restaurant with a seasonally-led menu to match.

Expect all the modern British classics with plenty of appealing, imaginative flavour combinations.

EBRINGTON

Ebrington Arms

Pubs/bars

Ebrington, near Chipping Campden,
Glos. GL55 6NH.
01386 593223.

Another excellent pub, all honeyed Cotswold stone, in a pretty village - just how lucky can this area get?

The Ebrington Arms feels like a proper pub too. The bar is complete with real fire and friendly natives; you can eat here (where inevitably, it can get a bit smoky) or choose the small but comfortable dining room. Either way, the food is very good, no-nonsense and done well using quality ingredients.

A starter of roast red pepper tart tasted as good as it looked and in a nice twist on the norm, the case was made of a prettily-shaped parmesan tuile.

Rack of lamb was excellent and came with a delicious dauphinoise of celeriac and sweet potato and a crepe parmentier with hollandaise and wild mushrooms was also a dish to write home about - the crepe made with potato rather than the usual batter.

This is an unassuming and welcoming treasure of a place.

EVESHAM

Wood Norton Hall

Fine dining

Wood Norton, Evesham, WR11 4YB.
www.wnhall.co.uk
01386 425780.

An imposing building and a beautifully swish dining room here are all very impressive.

This is definitely a place for a grand night out but the food doesn't really deserve the steep price tag - £37.50 for three courses. It's good but it's not that good.

Still, it has its fans and as a special occasion venue, it's worth considering if the flexible fiend is up to it.

FAWSLEY

Fawsley Hall

Fine dining

Fawsley, near Daventry, Northants, NN11 3BA.
www.fawsleyhall.com
01327 892000.

Just over the border from Warwickshire and nicely close to Althorp for Princess Diana fans, Fawsley Hall is an impressive stately pile - more a hamlet than a house, with its wealth of buildings.

It was restored from a near-ruin in the 1970s and although the aim is high luxury, it can have a bit of a corporate feel about it (it is a popular conference centre).

The food aims to impress and prices are high. Expect an offal lot of à la carte grandeur and serious prices, especially for wine.

GREAT WOLFORD

Fox and Hounds

Pubs/bars

Great Wolford, near Shipston-on-Stour, Warks, CV36 5NQ.
www.thefoxandhoundsinn.com
01608 674220.

A quintessential, honey-coloured Cotswold pub, the Fox and Hounds is perfectly sited for those who like to tick the requisite items off the perfect country pub checklist - stone-flagged floors, a real fire in a great inglenook fireplace and proper beams.

The classy but comforting food is modern rustic and kept fairly simple but flavours are well handled and truly appealing.

HADLEY HEATH

Hadley Bowling Green Inn

Pubs/bars

Hadley Heath, near Droitwich, Worcestershire, WR9 0AR.
www.hadleybowlinggreen.co.uk
01905 620294.

A very smartly-revamped pub in lovely Worcestershire countryside, the Hadley Bowling Green also boasts more than its fair share of history - the bowling green which gives it its name (and is still there) is apparently the UK's oldest and it's thought the gunpowder plotters used this as a meeting place.

They wouldn't recognise it now, of course. This is a very gastropub-style, with its stylish new look nicely embracing all the building's old features.

The food is seriously restaurant (there is in fact a separate non-smoking restaurant) and has prices to match. Very aspirational.

It famously once offered a squirrel and foie gras terrine among the starters. And it didn't even carry the warning 'may contain nuts'!

HAGLEY

Lyttelton Arms

Pubs/bars

Bromsgrove Road, Hagley, Worcestershire, DY9 9LJ. www.thelytteltonarms.co.uk 01562 882213.

The unstoppable Pauls Salisbury and Hales continue their joint Orange Tree venture with M&B apace. The Lyttelton Arms is one of the latest beneficiaries (opening in 2005) and one of the best.

Chic, beautifully-designed surroundings and great, unfussy, contemporary food make this place a winner. It's essential to book as it's already a huge success.

Va Bene

Italian

127 Worcester Road, Hagley, Stourbridge, DY9 0NW. 01562 882888.

Va Bene is a popular venue in little Hagley's bustling high street and that's no surprise - after all, Italian is the favourite cuisine of so many of us (and children too). And when it's served in stylish, modern surroundings like this, it's a winner for families, groups of mates or romantic couples alike.

The menu keeps it simple with a range of pizzas, pastas and risottos. Service is young and friendly.

West One

Pubs/bars

**159 Worcester Road, West Hagley,
Worcs, DY9 0NW.
01562 885328.**

Youthful and trendy, this stylish little bar and bistro has been a big hit and brings in visitors from miles around.

The food offers a general fusion of Med, Brit and touches of Thai. It's all pretty well done and there are acres of young, friendly staff to keep it all on track.

HAMBLETON

Hambleton Hall ★

Fine dining

**Hambleton, Oakham, Rutland, LE15 8TH.
www.hambletonhall.com
01572 756991.**

Hambleton Hall has a Michelin star thanks to its busy chef Aaron Paterson.

His intense care for ingredients is more than matched by technical skill and mastery of presentation.

But better than the food - amazingly - is the venue. Here is a glorious country house in fine grounds which gazes out on to beautiful Rutland Water (now home to breeding ospreys). It feels like an island - and one which manages to offer utter luxury but with no pomp, the perfect combination for any top flight restaurant and hotel.

HAMPTON-IN ARDEN

White Lion

Pubs/bars

**High Street, Hampton-in-Arden,
Solihull, B92 0AA.
01675 442833.**

There's some excellent, mainly Italian food on offer in the stylishly contemporary restaurant behind this pretty village pub.

Enjoy the nicely buzzy atmosphere as you tuck into some great bruschetta, tasty slow-roasted lamb shank with flageolet beans or some good cannelloni.

Freshness and a real generosity of spirit abounds in the food here.

Prices are much as you'd expect for gastro pub grub.

HENLEY-IN-ARDEN

Edmunds ★★

Modern British

**64 High Street, Henley-in-Arden,
Warks. B95 5BX.
01564 795666.**

Michelin-starred Andy Waters is chef-patron of this wonderful, bijou place in picturesque Henley-in-Arden.

Although the restaurant is only small, it's pretty, relaxed and very friendly but, it's the superb food which has them queuing up to book (Friday and Saturday nights are filled up months in advance).

When you finally get in, you'll understand why. This is truly delicious stuff but with no pretensions or unnecessary fripperies. And it's amazingly good value.

Vegetarians are well looked after too with their own menu of fab dishes; probably the best vegetarian food around in fact.

Matricardi's ★

Italian/European

97 High Street, Henley-in-Arden, Warks. B95 5AT.
www.matricardis.co.uk
01564 792135.

Matricardi's is something of a shock to the system.

Right in the middle of Henley's quaint and chintzy high street, it looks from the outside like a teeny little place but behind this bijou bar area, a lengthy corridor takes you along to a large and definitely swanky urban restaurant, all romantic lighting and smart leather chairs. There's even a lovely - and even larger - garden beyond.

The food is excellent too. There's a lot of Italian but also many contemporary European and even global touches; nothing too complex but all appealing and competently done.

Friendly service adds the perfect finishing touch.

I eat at this German-Chinese restaurant and the food is delicious. The only problem is that an hour later you're hungry for power.
Dick Cavett

HEREFORD

Cafe at All Saints

Vegetarian

**All Saints Church, High Street,
Hereford, HR4 9AA.**
www.cafeatallsaints.co.uk
01432 370415.

A fully-operational cafe in a church may seem somewhat bizarre; the fact that this is a vegetarian cafe with a licence - may seem odder still but the eaterie here is a little gem.

Bill Sewell, who runs the vegetarian restaurant The Place Below in London, is the cook behind the menu although the cafe's completely owned by the church, which also receives all the profits.

Hearty comfort is the guiding principle. Soups are thick enough to stand your spoon in, there'll be quiches, loaded no doubt with rustic cheeses, or maybe a Moroccan casserole with almond and currant bulghur.

Local produce plays a starring role whenever possible.

Castle House Hotel - La Rive restaurant ★

Fine dining

Castle Street, Hereford, HR1 2NW.
www.castlehse.co.uk
01432 356321.

Not many new places, not even ones as swish as this, would normally hope to pick up four AA rosettes in their first year.

But Castle House managed not just that but also scooped the title of AA hotel of the year.

Its record of success has continued too. This is true elegance; fine dining as it should be. An experience of such hedonism, it must be the hotel equivalent of a heavenly massage.

Prices, considering the league they're in, are actually quite sensible - but beware the cost of the wine.

Floodgates Brasserie

Modern British

**Left Bank Village, Bridge Street,
Hereford, HR4 9DG.
www.leftbank.co.uk
01432 349009**

Floodgates is the relaxed sibling to the fine dining of the Castle House hotel (see separate entry). Both are owned by, and the brainchild of, Dr Albert Heijn, a fabulously wealthy Dutch guy whose own estate in Hereford provides the livestock which ends up on all the menus.

Floodgates is part of the Left Bank village, a modern block right on the banks of the Wye which also houses decent food shops, a cafe and bar.

If the weather is fine, grab a table outside, whether just for a coffee or a chunky club sandwich or a hearty meal.

The service is solicitous but relaxed, the decor colourfully modern and the food reliably good quality and imaginative.

Where do you go to get anorexia?
Shelly Winters

HOCKLEY HEATH

Nuthurst Grange

Fine dining

**Nuthurst Grange Lane, Hockley Heath,
Warwickshire, B94 5NL.
www.nuthurst-grange.com
01564 783972.**

Barely more than a slip road's length from the M40 is
this fine country house hotel, all elegant grounds, squashy
sofas by roaring fires and big curtains.

Its restaurant is formal with an ambience of almost
unconcerned luxury.

Behind the ease, however, is a lot of graft, with the hard-
working kitchen offering homemade breads and petit
fours as well as the choice available in two set menus.

It is pricy, however, and whether the food is quite up to
the expense is doubtful.

The hotel has been under new ownership since
December 2004.

ILMINGTON

Howard Arms ★

Pubs/bars

**Lower Green, Ilmington,
near Shipston-on-Stour, Warks, CV36 4LT.
www.howardarms.com
01608 682226.**

You don't have to be a tourist to admire the Cotswold
perfection of this glorious stone-built, award-winning
place gazing over a little village green.

Grab a comfy chair and find a table (if you can) in the bar or snug or dining room of this civilised, award-winning free house and enjoy some fine ales along with some home-made, hearty treats by the real fire.

The menu is chalked up on a blackboard and there's an awful lot of tempting choices to wade through before you make your order at the bar.

There's plenty of rustic, hearty upmarket pub grub here but the approach is modern and adds lots of interesting tweaks. The veggie option is also top-notch and often nicely different from the norm.

The family also owns the Horse and Groom in Bourton on the Hill near Moreton-in-Marsh.

IVERLEY

Crown at Iverley

Pubs/bars

Norton Road, Iverley, Stourbridge, DY8 2RX. 01562 885533.

An ultra-smart modern pub for the smart set, the Crown at Iverley is proving a hit with its blend of modern flavours, quality ingredients and capable cooking.

The hearty meaty dishes are often the winners here, the fillet of beef with buttered greens and toasted goat's cheese - a star during the review meal.

There's also some decent charcuterie and nice homemade puds for those with any room left.

KENILWORTH

The Cross

Pubs/bars

16 New Street, Kenilworth, Warks, CV8 2EZ.
www.thecrossatkenilworth.co.uk
01926 853840.

A decidedly chic place, the Cross is a large pubby restaurant - or perhaps restauranty pub - with the feel in the main dining room of a well-to-do house.

This is a popular place but they have service down to a (pretty) fine art so even when the car park is full, as it often is, they can cope with the numbers.

Someone takes great care of the food here, with a menu that is innovative and full of quality ingredients. Choices for vegetarians are particularly good, from chick pea and potato spring rolls with halloumi and a tamarind dip to butternut and sage ravioli in walnut sauce. Quality stuff indeed and a pretty terrace and garden too.

Restaurant Bosquet ★

French

97a Warwick Road, Kenilworth,
Warks, CV8 1HP.
www.restaurantbosquet.co.uk
01926 852463.

Behind its English suburban home frontage, Restaurant Bosquet is a hive of Frenchness.

Perhaps it's all the fervour of an ex-pat that makes chef-patron Bernard Lignier run his business on such resoundingly Gallic lines.

The wine list is all French and the cooking is also French, although much if it is rustic in origin, cuisine de terroir rather than the cuisine of Michelin-starred grandeur - and as hugely flavoursome as that should imply.

Simply Simpsons ★

Modern British

**101/103 Warwick Road, Kenilworth,
Warks, CV8 1HL.
www.simplysimpsons.com
01926 864567.**

The old Simpsons' restaurant has now become a more informal, brasserie-style eaterie called Simply Simpsons.

It's as chic and smart as ever and though the food has become simpler - as the name would suggest - it's still top quality and is now fantastic value (cheaper than any gastropub).

Chef-patron Andreas Antona also has the fabulous Michelin-starred Simpsons Restaurant with Rooms in Birmingham but is determined that his original restaurant won't suffer as a result.

The change of style is a winner, service is as excellent as ever and the food - whether superb risottos or topnotch steaks - is outstanding. Check out the plats du jour which include trad classics such as Black Country faggots and steak and kidney pie. All beautifully done, naturally.

*When the waitress puts
the dinner on the table,
the old men look at the dinner.
The young men look at the waitress.*

Gelett Burgess

KNIGHTWICK

Talbot

Pubs/bars

Knightwick, Worcestershire, WR6 5PH.
www.the-talbot.co.uk
01886 821235.

Try a half of This, That or T'Other in this friendly, family-run pub - for these are the specialist beers created by Philip Clift who runs the Teme Valley Brewery out back while sisters Wiz and Anne deal with the hostelry side.

A family venture then, and a very popular one in this, one of the prettiest corners of Worcestershire, next door to Bromyard and by the snaking waters of the Teme.

There's a simply-lawned garden but unfortunately the river is out of sight, though so close to hand.

Service can be forgetful but it does get very busy.

KNOWLE

Loch Fyne

Seafood

Bank House, High Street, Knowle,
near Solihull, B93 0JU.
www.lochfyne.com
01564 732750.

A smart, airy and relaxed restaurant specialising in fish and seafood which also offers fishmongery and takeaways.

The food is modern, simple and appealing with bags of choice but omnivores and veggies need worry not - there are other options available (such as smoked Islay sausages or polenta gnocchi with gruyere and tomato) and they're just as delicious as the fish (to my mind).

Staff are young and matey and the whole place has a great feelgood ambience. Decent value too.

Spirals

Modern British

5 St Johns Way, Knowle, Solihull, B93 0LE.
01564 739395.

A chi chi, good-looking place, Spirals offers a rollcall of modern favourites which perfectly suits its colourful modern interior.

Here you can find such bistro regulars as crab and chilli cakes, lots of fish and plenty of pasta at reasonable prices.

It may not be in the top league but it's comforting, weighty stuff and it certainly fills a niche and gets a lot of local support.

LAPWORTH

The Boot

Pubs/bars

Old Warwick Road, Lapworth,
Warks, B94 6JU.
www.bootinnlapworth.co.uk
01564 782464.

The Boot is one of a handful of wonderful gastro pubs owned by Paul Salisbury and Paul Hales.

As with their other ventures, the look is spot-on, service is youthful, slick and friendly and the food is bang up to date and delicious.

This has long been a favourite local watering hole - a modest-looking roadside pub which has been well and truly Salisburyed.

The old peacefully cohabits with the new - nicely rustic furniture, tastefully paint-effected, the exposed beams are pale and interesting rather than painted black and hung with horse brasses.

The menu is very appealing, full of tantalising flavours with fresh ideas, novel taste combinations and a real sense of quality.

The Punchbowl

Pubs/bars

**Mill Lane, Lapworth, Warwickshire, B94 6HR.
01564 784564.**

Chic and stylish, the Punchbowl is one of the new breed of gastropubs, with an interior as large and stylish as its menu is ambitious.

In a beautifully rural spot, it ticks most of the boxes when it comes to a meal out.

The food is the global mix you'd expect and very carefully presented, although some dishes didn't quite match up on flavour.

LEAMINGTON SPA

Oscar's at 39

French

**39 Chandos Street, Leamington Spa, CV32 4RL.
www.aubreyallen.co.uk
01926 452807.**

A little corner of Leamington Spa that is forever France... Oscar's is a little gem of a place, a bistro that easily bears comparison with many of the French originals it is based on.

The menu is kept short, simple and classic - country paté or perhaps fishcakes among the starters, garlic pot-roasted lamb, coq au vin or some fine steaks among the mains (the venture is owned by the catering butchers par excellence Aubrey Allen, who also have a fine deli nearby, so expect superb meat).

These rustic and appealing dishes are cooked well and prices are eminently sensible - two courses cost £16 at dinner and £11 at lunch.

There's also a very popular 'auberge' night on Tuesdays where a single-choice three-course meal is only £12.50.

Solo

Modern British

23 Dormer Place, Leamington Spa.
01926 422422.

Solo's owner is Ian Wallace of the excellent Wykham
Arms near Banbury (see Sibford Gower).

This, his original place and first solo (geddit?) venture, is
up for sale but business is continuing as they await a buyer.

So grab the chance while you can to enjoy some great,
robust food in appealing (yet very bijou) surroundings.

LICHFIELD

Bratz

Modern British

Minster House, Pool Walk,
Lichfield, W13 6QT.
01543 253788

One of Lichfield's more recent ventures, this smart and
ambitious place overlooking scenic Minster Pool is the
workplace of up-and-coming chef Christopher Bratt-Rose.

He reached the regional finals of the Roux Scholarship
earier in 2004 and clearly wants to make his mark.

The food is confident and aspirational, whether it's a
starter of warm salad of guinea fowl or goat's cheese
bavarois.

Some dishes are more successful than others but it's
generally very good. A yellow pepper soup with tarragon
linguini and pot-roast lamb were particularly enjoyed,
a scallop risotto less so.

But there's imagination and quality on offer throughout
and the historic building is a delight. Certainly worth
a visit.

Chandlers Grande Brasserie

Modern British

Corn Exchange, Conduit Street, Lichfield, Staffs, WS13 6JU.
01543 416688.

Behind its elegantly brick-arched frontage, Chandlers offers even more attractive settings - you walk into a sizeable, wooden-floored bustling bar in the lobby from which a brass-railed staircase swings off to the left.

And through this is an airy atrium of a dining room with a high, domed ceiling bearing a huge chandelier.

The circular dining room is tastefully decorated and if space runs out here, there is a gallery offering more seating above it.

There can be service niggles but the food is generally of a decent brasserie standard.

Lloyds No 1

Pubs/bars

1 Bird Street, Lichfield, WS13 6PW.
www.lloydsno1.co.uk
01543 258525

Lloyds No 1 cafe bar is a chain which offers chain-type fare but of a reasonable standard and in a pleasant, cream-walled, pale-wooded environment.

The building, a clean-lined cream affair, is pretty imposing too. Robust, no-nonsense menu pleasers could travel the world, including everything from nachos (a filling selection for two) to Thai green chicken curry or a host of pasta dishes.

Oddfellows in the Boat

Pubs/bars

Walsall Road, Springhill, Lichfield, WS14 0BU.
01543 361692.

Seemingly undecided whether it's a pub or a restaurant or a pub in a restaurant, Oddfellows plays both cards with a wealth of food choice in a pubby environment.

Even with the number of dishes on offer, the quality is more than reasonable. Brie and red onion parcels were great, as was a fiery Cajun salmon though pheasant and pigeon were felt to be a tad overcooked.

Puds are delicious and prices not bad at all.

Olive Tree

Modern British

34 Tamworth Street, Lichfield. WS13 6JJ.
www.olivetreelichfield.co.uk
01543 263363.

There's no holding back with the trendy looks at this Mediterranean cafe and restaurant.

Chef-watchers will be happy to hear that they can see their meal being prepared in the open kitchen at the end of the room.

Chicken, fish and pasta are the mainstays.

Thai Rainbow

Thai

15 Bird Street, Lichfield.
01543 264209

If ever proof were need that Thai is one of our favourite cuisines these days, this place provides it in spades.

The crowds pack out this buzzy eaterie, hungry for good, authentic food at sensible prices. They leave happy and they keep coming back.

There's no need for a cool, minimalist decor either à la smart places in Birmingham. Thai Rainbow, right in the city centre, offers a traditionally over-the-top decor, all rich colours, ornate carvings and full-on furniture.

Friendly full-costumed service adds to the atmosphere.

Thrales

Modern British

40-44 Tamworth Street, Lichfield,
Staffordshire, WS13 6JJ.
www.thrales.co.uk
01543 255091.

The quaint old building that is home to Thrales restarant dates back to the 1600s and in its not-so-romantic past it used to be an abattoir.

Inside, it's now a cosy, homely sort of place with a menu that plays it pretty straight - maybe Charentais melon with prawns and marie rose dressing or stilton pate to start, followed by some good milk-fed pigeon or seabass.

Not all dishes have 100 per cent success rate but a good enough place on the whole.

LLANFAIR WATERDINE

The Waterdine ★

Pubs/bars

**Llanfair Waterdine, near Knighton,
Shropshire, LD7 1TU.
www.waterdine.com
01547 528214.**

The term gastro-pub could have been invented for this place (which has a Michelin Bib Gourmand).

Ken and Isabel Adams moved here from the Oaks restaurant in Ludlow (now Hibiscus, see separate entry).

It's a simply glorious and remote spot on the banks of the Teme and must have one of the best views around.

A bar menu offers excellent, simpler fare but the fine dining restaurant food is just superb and well-priced.

The 16th century black and white longhouse has some interesting tales to tell - mainly that Mallory planned his fateful Everest expedition in the bar. Pretty rooms available.

LOWER QUINTON

College Arms ★

Pubs/bars

**Lower Quinton, near Stratford-upon-Avon.
www.collegearms.co.uk
01789 720342**

A superb new venture from the 2004 National Chef of the Year Steve Love, a top regional talent to celebrate.

This ancient, beamed pub has been smartly modernised and is now the epitome of gastro elegance, all chocolate leather seating and smart tables.

Food is currently just served in Henry's Bar (named in honour of Henry VIII, who once owned the place) but there are plans for a fine dining restaurant in the autumn of 2005.

Expect some stunning dishes, with top quality ingredients and first-class cooking. This is not what would normally pass as bar food - here, you'll find gourmet delights at sensible prices.

LOWER SLAUGHTER

Lower Slaughter Manor

Fine dining

Lower Slaughter, near Bourton-on-the-Water, Glos, GL54 2HP.
www.lowerslaughter.co.uk
01451 820456.

This magnificent country house is set in an impossibly-pretty village near Bourton-on-the-Water. (Within a minute's drive is the equally-stunning Upper Slaughter, home to Lords of the Manor).

The food is good, safe and classic offered in excellent surroundings and served by attentive staff.

A textbook place for those prepared to pay the premium it commands.

LUDLOW

Courtyard

Modern British

2 Quality Square, Ludlow, SY8 1AR.
www.thecourtyard-ludlow.co.uk
01584 878080.

Ludlow doesn't just have the Michelin-starred joints with the months-long queues to get in, it also has little gems like the Courtyard, a modest place with bare pine tables and a neat, housewifely interior that lives in the cobbled, delightfully-named Quality Square.

The home-cooked fare emerging from the open-plan kitchen is interesting and pleasantly satisfying. This is the place where the locals go.

Hibiscus ★★

Modern French

17 Corve Street, Ludlow, SY8 1DA.
www.hibiscusrestaurant.co.uk
01584 872325.

The blessed Ludlow is particularly lucky to host the first independent outing of the precociously-talented Frenchman Claude Bosi. And with the decison of Michelin in 2004 to promote him to two stars, he is at last getting the status he deserves.

He is an outstanding chef - even in this area, with all the amazing competition. With wife Claire running a serene and friendly front of house, he has brought an easy, stylishly modern look into these olde worlde surroundings.

Claude's cooking has an exquisite lightness and artistry which never fails to surprise. This is food which manages extraordinary depths and complexities of flavour and yet is almost ethereal.

Request vegetarian options in advance.

Mr Underhill's ★★

Modern British

Dinham Weir, Ludlow, SY8 1EH.
www.mr-underhills.co.uk
01584 874431.

One of my all-time favourite restaurants, Michelin-starred Mr Underhill's beautiful riverside setting and sublime food have made it a top destination.

The friendly "restaurant with rooms" sits splendidly below Ludlow Castle and famously offers a single-option menu. Losing the option of choice, though, is no sacrifice with food as first-class and intensely-flavoured as this.

If the suggested menu doesn't suit, alternatives (including vegetarian options) can be discussed in advance.

MALVERN

Cottage in the Wood

Modern British

Holywell Road, Malvern Wells, WR14 4LG.
www.cottageinthewood.co.uk
01684 575859.

It is the stunning view here which has hungry diners regularly making the trek to Malvern.

From this cosy hotel tucked high up on the hillside, an immense vista lies out before you, a glorious vision of rural England at its most beautiful. It looks magnificent by day and magical by night.

It is a family-run and comfortable hotel, very eager to please and with a great wine list at sensible prices.

MERIDEN

Manor Hotel

Fine dining

Main Road, Meriden, Warks, CV7 7NH.
www.manorhotelmeriden.co.uk
01676 522735.

A lovely Georgian hotel with a rather swanky, be-swagged dining room, the Manor Hotel boasts Peter Griffiths as its head chef - the head of the British Culinary Federation, no less, and a leading figure in the trade.

The food is pretty formal, as you might expect, but there are contemporary flavours mixed in with the luxury ingredients. Some superb scallops with black pudding, pea puree and port sauce hit the right note, as did a breast of duck with apple fondant, caramelised endive and cassis sauce.

Not all dishes were quite such barnstormers, notably a rather bland souffle, but generally the Manor hits a solid, reliable note and is a local favourite for special occasion dining.

NOTTINGHAM

Restaurant Sat Bains★★

Modern British

Old Lenton Lane, Nottingham, NG27 2SA.
www.restaurantsatbains.net
0115 9866566.

Sat Bains' star is truly in the ascendant and his great talent has been honoured with a Michelin star.

He deserves even more. Sat is a chefs' chef and his cooking is seriously impressive. Try the gourmet tasting menu and be prepared for course after course of sublime little moments for your tastebuds. Only the best ingredients are used here and there are always plenty of surprises. This is not a chef who rests on his laurels.

Not that you're likely to go wrong with anything here in these chic surroundings. It may be a something of a trek but more than worth the effort.

OLDBURY

Wing Wah

Oriental

**188 Causeway Green Road,
Oldbury, B68 8LQ.
www.wingwah.net
0121 552 0041.**

After their great success on the Wing Yip estate in Nechells, the Wing Wah team have added another string to their bow with this massive place in Oldbury.

What was once the Hen and Chickens pub is now a thriving little outpost of Chinatown. The food doesn't go for the à la carte authentic thrills of the original WW though, for here a giant, junk-shaped bar serves up one of the best value bargain buffets around.

The choice is massive (if restricted for vegetarians) and includes a Japanese teppenyaki table with suitable amounts of flame as well as a selection of satay, tempura and Thai curries.

It gets very busy and appeals hugely to the ravenous budget-watcher.

OLTON

Rajnagar International

Indian

256 Lyndon Road, Olton, Solihull, B92 7AW.
www.rajnagar.com
0121 742 8140/4842.

The quality-driven Rajnagar is one of the thoroughly reliable Indian restaurants that dot the land.

The look of the interior has been brought up to date and the food is good quality, with lots of fish. It's a particular strength here - the monkfish massala is particularly worth trying.

An elder sibling to Barajee on Broad Street, Birmingham.

OMBERSLEY

Cross Keys

Pubs/bars

Main Street, Ombersley,
Worcestershire, WR9 0DS.
01905 620588.

Despite the preponderance of eateries in this small village (two other food pubs and a restaurant), the Cross Keys more than holds its own.

Loyal regulars love this comfortable, traditionally pubby place, with beams, hopbines, dark wood tables and fires and they keep it busy.

Food is its main focus and there's plenty to choose from, with a lengthy menu and a blackboard of specials over the bar.

Crown and Sandys Arms

Pubs/bars

Main Road, Ombersley, Worcs. WR9 0EW.
www.crownandsandys.co.uk
01905 620252.

It's a popular place, the Crown and Sandys, both with loyal locals and those who like a drive out to a pretty village (and Ombersley is certainly that).

Inside the rather grand white building (which always reminds me of a little of an old cinema) there's a cosy bar and two dining rooms.

The focus is very much on the bistro-style food and though it can be patchy (is this long menu simply too much to offer?), it's generally pretty good and most people trying it tend to go back.

Venture In ★

Modern British

Main Road, Ombersley, Worcs, WR9 0EW.
01905 620552.

The Venture In's chef-patron Toby Fletcher worked at the neighbouring Crown and Sandys before deciding to set up for himself at this quaint and pretty black and white restaurant.

And very successful he's been too. The bijou place has a smart, modern look inside which blends well with the ancient beams, inglenook fireplace and old stone.

The cooking here can be a bit of a blow-out but it's jampacked with flavour. Toby excels at intensifying the taste in every ingredient. It's good value too.

ONIBURY

Apple Tree

Cafe/bar

**Onibury, near Craven Arms,
Shropshire, SY7 9AW.
01584 856633.**

Just off the A49 Ludlow to Craven Arms road is this little gem of a cafe bar.

It's a down to earth, small place, a mix of pub and bistro in style which makes the most of excellent local produce.

Try the excellent, tasty salads or soups, or perhaps local sausages and mash or griddled neck lamb chops. Good local beers and ciders too.

> *How is education supposed to make me feel smarter? Besides, every time I learn something new, it pushes some old stuff out of my brain. Remember when I took that home winemaking course and I forgot how to drive?*
>
> Homer Simpson

PAXFORD

Churchill Arms

Pubs/bars

**Paxford, near Chipping Campden,
Glos, GL55 6XH.
www.thechurchillarms.com
01386 594000.**

In this tiny village, top chef Sonya Kidney's neat, unassuming stone pub looks rather unremarkable considering its fierce gastro reputation.

Inside, it can be a bit on the cheek-by-jowl side but the look is pleasant and informal - just the right sort of blend of trendy and tradition.

The menu - chalked up on a blackboard on a central pillar of the pub - fires on all cylinders of a hot-wired foodie imagination.

It gets very, very busy but they take care to make sure the drinking locals are not excluded by diners.

PERSHORE

Belle House ★

Modern British

**Bridge Street, Pershore, Worcs, WR10 1AJ.
www.belle-house.co.uk
01386 555055.**

Pershore is a lovely old town and it deserves a smart eaterie like this (which also houses a good traiteur).

The Belle House's wonderfully tall windows look out on to the bustling main street and add panache to an interior which is already smart and elegantly contemporary.

A good value menu offers a rollcall of tempting modern flavours, whether it's succulent shoulder of lamb braised with rosemary and thyme served with roast new potatoes and swede puree or a fabulously flavoursome herb gnocchi with parmesan, creme fraiche and wilted rocket.

The restaurant has now been bought out by head chef Steve Waits who runs the show with sous chef Sue Ellis, a former winner of the Midlands Young Chef of the Year competition.

PRESTON BAGOT

Crabmill ★

Pubs/bars

Preston Bagot, Claverdon, Warks, B95 5DR.
www.thecrabmill.co.uk
01926 843342.

One of the best pubs around for food - and also one of the best-looking.

Trendy is definitely the name of the game (like its siblings the Boot at Lapworth and the Orange Tree at Chadwick End) but there's no question of style over substance - the food is most certainly on a par with the decor and round here, that's a big compliment.

As for the food, it could be offered on prescription for those with a jaded palate.

This is pub grub to blow the cobwebs away - youthful and vibrant, casual but chic, comforting yet zippily fresh.

PRIORS HARDWICK

Butchers Arms

Pubs/bars

**Priors Hardwick, near Southam,
Warks, CV47 7SN.
www.thebutchersarms.com
01327 260504.**

There are strong Portuguese links at this beamed and
horse-brassed ancient inn which is now far more of a
restaurant than a pub.

That's mainly thanks to co-owner Lino, a blazered, suave
Portuguese guy running a terribly-attentive front of house.

But the country's influence is also in evidence in the
big menu. Among the generous, well-cooked and
hearty roster of dishes are lots of "langoustinhos" and
Portuguese rice pudding (which is excellent).

Otherwise, it's a more familiar roll call of lamb shank,
pastas and so on. It may seem a little dated but it's an
efficient and highly successful operation.

ROWINGTON

The Wood ★

Pubs/bars

**Finwood Road, Rowington,
Warwickshire, CV35 7DH.
www.thewoodatrowington.co.uk
01564 782252.**

The Wood - a "country restaurant and bar" - offers excellent quality and good value food in smartly-refurbished surroundings.

The 150-year-old building (formerly known as Tom o'the Wood) is also in a great spot, nicely rural and with the Grand Union canal for anyone who fancies a towpath stroll to walk off lunch.

It's a good lunch (or dinner) too, with chef Wayne Thomson (formerly of the Welcombe Hotel in Stratford and Nailcote Hall) at the helm. Very good value.

SELLACK

Loughpool Inn

Pubs/bars

**Sellack, Ross-on-Wye,
Herefordshire, HR9 6LX.
01989 730236.**

An idyllic country pub deep in lovely Herefordshire. Former chef-patron Steve Bull has now moved on but the place is still worth tracking down as there's decent food to be sampled under its aged beams.

Big hearty flavours are the order of the day with good ingredients simply treated to let the flavours shine through unencumbered.

SHATTERFORD

Dominiques

Pubs/bars

Bellmans Cross Inn, Bridgnorth Road, Shatterford, near Bewdley, DY12 1RN. 01299 861322.

Dominiques is actually the restaurant side of a pub and though it may be in deepest Worcestershire, there's an overwhelmingly French influence going on, thanks to the French landlord and chef - the eponymous Dominique.

The food is substantial but also shows some nice touches of ambition. Mains are strong on the big and meaty and have well turned-out garnishes. The wine list is good and offers non-French favourites.

SHREWLEY

Durham Ox

Pubs/bars

Shrewley Common, Shrewley, Near Warwick, Warwickshire CV35 7AY.
www.durham-ox.com
01926 842283.

Shrewley is a small village and rather tucked away but this place is definitely worth seeking out.

It's a big old pub given a stylish but comfortable modern rustic feel. The dining room feels very much the main hub of the place rather than a soulless add-on and has a relaxed and buzzy atmosphere.

They care about food here and do it well. The menu offers many of today's popular choices - lamb shank, cod and chips, ribeye steak et al - but with top quality ingredients, they really are something special.

It's informal but quality fare - served by friendly and helpful staff - that really hits the spot.

SIBFORD GOWER

Wykham Arms ★

Pubs/bars

Temple Mill Road, Sibford Gower, Banbury, Oxon. OX15 5RX.
www.wykhamarms.co.uk
01295 788808

The chef-patron of this quaint pub in a pretty village 20 miles south of Stratford-upon-Avon is self-trained Ian Wallace, who also still runs Solo restaurant in Leamington Spa (although it is for sale).

His is a talent worth following and this picturesque place is a great home for it.

Amid the ancient and smart surroundings, there is food here more than worth the journey. Try an excellent roasted Mediterranean vegetable salad or hearty soup followed by Brixham bream or excellent steaks.

There's plenty of support for quality regional produce too, from the Lighthorne lamb to the Simmental/Hereford cross beef.

SOLIHULL

Beau Thai

Thai

**761 Old Lode Lane, Solihull,
West Midlands, B92 8JE.
0121 743 5355. Fax 0121 688 5568.**

This old favourite of the Thai-loving crowd now has a new, rather more genteel, clubby look replacing its ornate flowery style of old.

But its many faithful regulars will be happy to know that the food in this upmarket interior is as good and genuinely authentic as ever, served by staff who are helpful and reassuringly friendly.

This venue was for sale as we went to print.

Metro Bar and Grill

Pubs/bars

**680-684 Warwick Road, Solihull.
www.metrobarandgrill.co.uk
0121 705 9495.**

Birmingham's ever-popular Metro now has this baby sibling in downtown, affluent Solihull.

The style is just as smart as you'd expect - all leather sofas and oak floors with a big curved bar dominating the room.

The food is full of bright flavours - both classical (prawn cocktail, cottage pie, steak and chips) and modern bistro (salads, duck confit, ham hock terrine). Generally very well done all of it, and a pleasantly buzzy and chic atmosphere to boot.

Yellow River

Chinese

**43 Mill Lane Arcade, Touchwood Centre,
Solihull, B91 3GS.
0121 711 6969.**

This vibrantly-colourful and relaxed Ken Hom-backed
place is perfectly sited for shoppers and cinema-goers at
the splendid Touchwood Centre.

A wide range of eastern delicacies is available - try one of
the bento boxes if you fancy a variety of tasty nibbles to
recharge your energies before another retail blitz.

Service is efficient and the food is reliably decent quality
as well as well-priced. It's also surprisingly smart for a
venue which styles itself a cafe.

STOURBRIDGE

French Connection

French

**3 Coventry Street, Stourbridge,
West Midlands, DY8 1EP.
01384 390940.**

Down one of busy little Stourbridge's side streets is this
humble little bistro with deli attached. Both are worth
a visit.

French Connection has obviously been modelled on a
French cafe and it works, with its little, red, gingham-
topped tables, red-striped walls and ceiling fans.

A bit cramped (and nearly always busy with hungry
shoppers) but it has a good feel and an authentic whiff of
garlic. Dishes are rustic and appealing.

Pedmore House

Modern British

Ham Lane, Pedmore, Stourbridge, DY9 0YA.
www.pedmorehouse.co.uk
01384 393132

The Highlander is the Pedmore House's deeply-traditional first floor restaurant, all tartan, watercolours of misty glens and clan bric-a-brac.

It's a comfortable, thoroughly reliable sort of place. Don't let the laminated menu cause you undue concern - this is generally good quality food in portions that would leave trenchermen begging for mercy.

If you're after somewhere deeply trendy, this ain't the place but for a good, old-fashioned blowout, it's a winner.

Seven Stars

Pubs/bars

Brook Road, Stourbridge, DY8 1NQ.
01384 444123

Only unveiled in its new incarnation at the end of 2004, the Seven Stars is the swankily-refurbished 'old rothole' as it was once known, something of a Stourbridge legend opposite the Junction railway station.

Now it's a thoroughly modern set-up, with a menu that reads like a greatest hits list of current gastropub favourites - lots of pizzas and pastas, risottos and hearty ciabatta sarnies.

Young, friendly service and a smart interior are adding to its popularity.

Tuscano

Italian

**Pedmore House, Ham Lane, Pedmore,
Stourbridge, DY9 0YA.
www.pedmorehouse.co.uk
01384 393132.**

A traditional retro-style Italian restaurant, Tuscano
occupies the basement of the Pedmore House where it
does very nicely, thank you.

Locals flock here for authentic and exceptionally well-
priced fare including lots of pasta, pizzas and some good
vegetable dishes.

A very efficient operation means something of a rapid-fire
service but nobody really minds fast food when it's like this.

STOURTON

The Fox Inn

Pubs/bars

**Bridgnorth Road, Stourton, near Stourbridge,
West Midlands, DY7 5BL.
01384 87771**

A smart white pub in a particularly pretty corner of the
countryside, the Fox has numerous advantages, not least
its huge garden, good views and smart little bistro.

There's a little conservatory too next door to the bar and
a mass of food on offer with a big blackboard list of dishes
in the bar and another menu for the bistro, though you
can mix and match.

STOW-ON-THE-WOLD

Hamiltons

Modern British

**Park Street, Stow-on-the-Wold,
Glos, GL54 1AQ.
01451 831700.**

Hamiltons looks rather like a little bit of Habitat suddenly descended on Agatha Christie territory but somehow it all seems to work.

Stow is a glorious Cotswold town with plenty of tea shops, antique shops and traditional pubs and, of course, what it really needed was a bang-up-to-date brasserie with streamlined pale wood, bare stone walls, zingy modern fusion cuisine and cutting-edge stylish china and cutlery.

A lively youthful imagination here takes expected centre stage. Fine, friendly service and a good wine list all add to the sense of bonhomie.

STRATFORD-UPON-AVON

Coconut Lagoon

Indian

**21 Sheep Street, Stratford-upon-Avon,
Warks, CV37 6RN.
www.coconutlagoon.com
01789 293546.**

Southern Indian food cooked well and served in vibrantly-colourful surroundings. See also the entry for the Birmingham sibling.

Embargo

Pubs/bars

**1 Shakespeare Street, Stratford-upon-Avon,
Warks, CV37 6RN.
01789 262233.**

Busy and buzzy, this throbbing bar/restaurant in Stratford
is a big hit with the younger crowd.

The food is just as youthful and lively. It may not all
score 100 per cent but it's good enough to make for an
enjoyable, if rather loud, night.

The One Elm

Pubs/bars

**1 Guild Street, Stratford-upon-Avon,
CV37 6QZ.
www.peachpubs.com
01789 404919.**

A sibling of the Rose and Crown in Warwick and even
smarter in decor, the One Elm is a bustling, modern place
which rightly attracts a crowd.

Expect some competently-cooked gastropub classics -
fishcakes, 'sausage of the week' with mash, pork cutlet,
cod and chips - all tasty fare and well-presented.

If the bar is too busy, there's an upstairs dining room and
a small garden too.

The Opposition

Modern British

**13 Sheep Street, Stratford, Warks, CV37 6EF.
01789 269980.**

The Opposition may be an old stager on the Stratford scene but its relaxed approach is a popular one still for natives as well as tourists.

Blackboards reel off a list of predominantly Med-based favourites designed for mid-priced appeal.

Russons

Modern British

**8 Church Street, Stratford, Warks, CV37 6HB.
01789 268822.**

One of those traditional tea shop-looking places, Russons keeps its many regulars more than happy with reliably cooked and tasty fare.

Thoroughly respectable it may be but you may still find yourself surprised by the more-than-acceptable cooking, even with the volume of choice available.

The Vintner

Modern British

**4-5 Sheep Street, Stratford, Warks, CV37 6EF.
www.the-vintner.co.uk
01789 297259.**

A well-known and well-established brasserie in a wonderfully quirky, 400-year-old building.

The food is a decent mix of modern classics competently done and it's a relaxing place to linger with friends over some very good coffee.

Welcombe Hotel

Fine dining

Warwick Road, Stratford CV37 0NR.
www.menzies-hotels.co.uk
01789 298598

These are more settled times for the unfeasibly grand Welcombe Hotel just outside Stratford-upon-Avon.

Years past have seen rapid personnel changes but things have been more settled since Menzies took over.

The food fits the impressive, heavily-panelled and high-ceilinged surroundings. This is ambitious, formal, cheffy stuff, fancily presented and prepared with great care and ability. Portions are well-judged and balanced.

The dining room has even more to offer - fantastic views across formal gardens and over the golf course and beyond. You can even enjoy coffee on the terrace while watching golfers tee off into the lake.

The West End

Pubs/bars

Bull Street, Stratford-upon-Avon,
Warwickshire CV37 6DT.
01789 268832.

Hidden away in the quaint small streets of old Stratford, this lively place comes as something of a surprise.

The Tardis-like interior is bigger than you'd expect and (mostly) modern but very comfortable with it.

There's plenty of choice with the food, from seared scallops with black pudding to lamb kofta, red Thai vegetable curry and haddock and chips. Daily specials add to the options.

It's all pretty good too, the only disappointment on an inspection visit being a bland vegetarian pasta dish. Everything else was fine.

STUDLEY

The Indonesian

Indonesian

**73 Alcester Road, Studley, Warks, B80 7NJ.
01527 857207.**

This is one of those restaurants where first appearances are decidedly deceptive.

The exterior is hardly welcoming and the layout wins it no friends but the tastes on offer, however, are something special.

A delicate combination of spice and fruit wins rave reviews - one great fan says it's the best Indonesian food he's tasted outside Indonesia (and Amsterdam). Service can be slow if they're busy.

McKees

Modern British

**8 Marble Alley, Studley,
Warwickshire, B80 7LD.
01527 853964.**

Tucked away down a tiny side street in this busy village is a real find.

McKees is a thoroughly friendly place adored by its regulars. On offer is reliably decent fare in a cosy, if slightly old-fashioned, environment

New Hall Hotel

Fine dining

Walmley Road, Sutton Coldfield, B76 1QX.
www.thistlehotels.com
0121 378 2442.

For those who want to push the boat out in credit card-hammering style, this could well be the perfect place.

New Hall is a gorgeous, listed, moated hotel but the food, while consummately stylish and superbly presented, has had its critics, who find it rather insubstantial and too nouvelle cuisine-ish for the considerable amount of money it costs.

Pier 39

Modern British

290-292 Lichfield Road, Mere Green,
Sutton Coldfield, B74 2UG.
www.pier-39.co.uk
0121 323 4600.

A big stylish place that often packs them in, Pier 39 can have bags of buzzy atmosphere despite being a little hit and miss in the food department.

The intentions are good - the menu reels off a list of modern, hearty food - but an occasional heavy-handedness can spoil things.

Place 2B

Pubs/bars

**Chester Road, Sutton Coldfield,
West Midlands, B73 5BD.
0121 354 8228.**

This mega pub (formerly Saints and Sinners) has had a complete new look and transformed itself into a sleek and thoroughly modern bar-restaurant.

The stylish, contemporary look is spot-on and the place has a good buzz.

Foodwise, it covers the right bases with lots of global influences, but there were a few hiccups on an inspection meal - scallops not properly trimmed for instance - that you wouldn't expect in this price bracket. The service was also rather untrained, although very friendly.

If it can polish up those rough edges, it should be on to a winner.

SWINFEN
....

Four Seasons restaurant at Swinfen Hall Hotel ★

Fine dining

**Swinfen, near Lichfield, Staffs, WS14 9RS.
www.swinfenhallhotel.co.uk
01543 481494.**

It's easy to imagine yourself in some gracious period TV drama as you drive up to this picturebook mansion.

This is grand living on a grand scale - huge rooms with huge windows and huge curtains and huge sofas.

Despite the obvious air of luxury, the approachable staff are down to earth and the food is satisfying too, classically based of course, although with contemporary touches.

TANWORTH-IN-ARDEN

The Bell

Pubs/bars

**The Green, Tanworth-in-Arden, Solihull,
Warks, B94 5AL.
www.thebellattanworthinarden.co.uk
01564 742212.**

A traditional village pub (and what a village - it's gorgeous) has been turned into a show-stopping gastro venture by a guy with an excellent local foodie pedigree - he launched Primitivo in Birmingham and West One in Hagley.

It looks good and by golly, the food's good too - and served in generous portions.

There are some delicious global goodies here, from Arabic mezze (wonderful dips) and seared Scottish scallops with chorizo to hefty lamb shank with mint jus and champ potato.

TITLEY

The Stagg Inn ★

Pubs/bars

**Titley, Kington, Herefordshire, HR5 3RL.
www.thestagg.co.uk
01544 230221.**

In the middle of this most rural of counties, the Stagg Inn struck a tremendous national first - the only pub in Britain to be awarded a coveted Michelin star.

It's a great pat on the back for the talented cooking of Roux brothers-trained chef-owner Steve Reynolds.

His menus are grounded in the excellent produce of the region - Marches beef, lamb, marvellous cheeses. Meat and poultry is often organic and/or free range.

Always busy - and rightly so - the place hasn't lost its pubby feel and has a great atmosphere.

ULLINGSWICK

Three Crowns ★

Pubs/bars

Ullingswick, Herefordshire, HR1 3JQ.
01432 820279.

Down a beautiful country lane, the Three Crowns plies its trade quietly and without fuss. Yet the food on offer here is wonderful and has won it awards for its celebration of excellent local produce.

The menu will depend on what is seasonally available and/or at its best. Whatever it is, without too much tampering, chef-patron Brent Castle will turn it into a delicious dish to be chalked up on the blackboard which dominates one wall in this quaint, hopbine-decorated little pub.

If the weather is fine, do sit outside - not only is it pretty, it is also quiet. Forget taped music or the drone of constant traffic, here you can actually hear the birds sing.

A marvellous place - it's just a shame that most of us will have to use our cars to get there.

UPPER SLAUGHTER

Lords of the Manor ★★

Fine dining

Upper Slaughter, near Bourton-on-the-Water, Glos, GL54 2JD.
www.lordsofthemanor.com
01451 820243.

Lords of the Manor has a history of fine food. Expect exceptionally-accomplished dishes with spot-on flavour combinations and all the class and style required in a joint like this.

It's all at the price range you'd expect, of course, but this is in the higher strata of eating out, a real special occasion venue.

Their chef is the criminally-underrated Les Rennie, formerly of Ynyshir Hall, and the cosy, calm dining room is a fine backdrop for his considerable talents. Go on - treat yourself.

WARWICK

Art Kitchen ★

Thai/Spanish

7 Swan Street, Warwick, CV34 4BJ.
www.theartkitchen.com
01926 494303.

A fabulously modern, arty little place serving great Thai food. It may be small but it's certainly perfectly formed, welcoming and comfortable.

But it's the food that makes the visit here so worthwhile - fresh, vibrant, zinging Thai flavours that give the tastebuds a great wake-up call.

If Thai's not your thing, there's also tapas on offer late afternoon.

Findons

Fine dining

7 Old Square, Warwick, CV34 4RA.
www.findons-restaurant.co.uk
01926 411755.

Chef-patron Michael Findon' eponymous restaurant is in a superb 18th century townhouse tucked away in a splendid square by the church in the centre of this lovely town.

It's fine dining but all is relaxed class, mellow and friendly. The cooking is modern in outlook but solidly grounded in technique and labour intensiveness. A lot of care goes on here and it's clear both in presentation and the scope of the menu.

Rose and Crown

Pubs/bars

30 Market Place, Warwick, CV34 4SH.
www.peachpubs.co.uk
01926 411117

The Rose and Crown, a bustling gastro pub in the heart of this historic town, has a lot to offer. It's buzzy and lively, often packed to the gills, and has great contemporary easy-eating food.

In its trendy stripped-floor and chunky tables interior, there are lots of lively ideas which border on the whimsical. There are "deli boards" on offer (as nibbles, a starter or to share), to be stacked up from a choice of cheese, charcuterie, antipasti and fish. You can get coffee, cakes and bacon sarnies to take away if you're pushed for time. And coffees come with a little bowl of Smarties rather than mint chocolates.

It's all very youthful and fun, and fast-moving, efficient staff mean you don't feel neglected despite the place's popularity.

Of course, what keeps people coming back is the quality of the hearty, crowd-pleasing food. There are great home-made faggots with mushy peas, onion gravy and chips or mash, excellent quality ribeye steaks, confit duck, fishcakes et al - typical gastro pub fare and done very well.

Saxon Mill

Pubs/bars

Coventry Road, Guys Cliffe,
Warwick, CV34 5YN.
www.saxonmill.co.uk
01926 492255.

The joint venture between Pauls Salisbury and Hales and M&B is another winner.

Sleek, modern and comfortable, this is the sort of youthful joint that's user-friendly for all age groups and is bound to become another destination place.

With pizzas, lots of pasta and a good list of such contemporary classics as duck confit, ribeye steak and seabass, the menu hits all the right buttons.

It's another Orange Tree venture (the original is in Chadwick End - not too far away) and if you know that, you'll have a good idea of the sort of informal but quality stuff that's on offer.

Where these guys always score highly is on atmosphere. There's always a good buzz about their places and this is no exception. Service is young and matey and it is a dream in summer with pretty tables outside overlooking the river.

WELFORD-ON-AVON

The Bell

Pubs/bars

Binton Road, Welford-on-Avon, Warks, CV37 8EB.
www.thebellwelford.co.uk
01789 750353.

Crowds pile into this smart, friendly place from miles around for food that is decent, homemade and down to earth.

The Bell also goes out of its way to support local producers, with a menu that credits many of them.

It's a large building with a pretty conservatory-style dining room to boot and it seems to fill the space with ease.

The comforting, homely fare on offer may include deep dish lasagne, scrumpy beef and tomato casserole and minty lamb curry - as well as traditional favourites such as fish and chips and sirloin steaks.

WINCHCOMBE

Five North Street ★

Modern British

**5 North Street, Winchcombe,
Glos, GL54 5LH.
01242 604566.**

Michelin-starred 5 North Street is an absolute gem in a pretty village to boot (with Sudeley Castle just round the corner too).

The restaurant is a cosy place, nicely done out and all ancient beams and dark wood tables and as for the food - well, it's just superb.

Chef-owner Marcus Ashenford used to run the kitchen at Chavignol at the Old Mill in Shipston-on-Stour so his pedigree is beyond doubt.

Here, doing his own thing with wife Kate running front of house, he concentrates on straightforward, deeply-flavoursome dishes which are confident and deceptively sophisticated, yet with nothing over-complicated or too cheffy.

A truffle risotto was sheer heaven, as were a savoy cabbage parcel of Chinese-style veg and braised pig's cheek, served with parsley mash and onion and sage confit.

Great vegetarian choice and sensible prices for the quality.

Wesley House ★

Modern British

High Street, Winchcombe, Glos. GL54 5LJ.
www.wesleyhouse.co.uk
01242 602366

The home of this excellent restaurant is a charming 15th century building on the chintzy high street.

A small bar and lounge (with a big log fire) leads through to a prettily-traditional dining room.

Cooking is sound and generous with the emphasis on generosity and variety. There's a sure hand in the kitchen here and the result is top quality, delicious fare.

WISHAW

The Belfry ★

Fine dining

The French Restaurant, the De Vere Belfry,
Wishaw, Sutton Coldfield. B76 9PR.
www.devereonline.co.uk
01675 470301

Now with ex-Bank wizard Idris Caldora in charge of all its foodie operations, the Belfry is offering superb fare in its French Restaurant.

The rollcall of superb dishes includes seared scallops with fennel barigoule, peppered lamb loin with pommes mousseline, braised pork shoulder with sage and fried fillet of beef with foie gras and truffle.

Luxury stuff indeed but with the expertise here, the confidence and ambition easily pays off.

Cock Inn

Pubs/bars

**Bulls Lane, Wishaw,
Sutton Coldfield, B76 9QL.
www.cockinnwishaw.co.uk
0121 313 3960.**

Another trendy gastro country pub from the same stable as the Boot at Lapworth and the Orange Tree at Chadwick End if perhaps not quite up to their league foodwise.

Still, it has a gorgeously trendy and upmarket interior and lots of appealing food, from pizzas to rib eye steaks and tasty pastas. There's innovation and nice global twists and turns aplenty.

WOLVERHAMPTON

Bilash Tandoori ★★

Bangladeshi

**2 Cheapside, Wolverhampton. WV1 1TU.
www.bilash-tandoori.co.uk
01902 427762. Fax: 01902 311991.**

When it comes to Bilash, I'm a bit of a bore. I sing its praises to all and sundry because I believe it leaves all other Indian restaurants standing.

The only pain factor involved in a Bilash trip is the (for me) long drive to Wolverhampton. (Others visit regularly from as far afield as the Cotswolds).

The restaurant now has an ultra-modern and beautiful interior on two floors and the food is even more impressive, winning chef-patron Sitab Khan many accolades over the years.

There is real passion, enormous commitment and equally enormous amounts of hard labour, happily done.

They grind and mix their own spices and many of the excellent ingredients - fresh curry leaves, huge prawns, fresh mangoes to name but three - are specially imported by another branch of the family.

Brown's

Modern British

24 Quay Street, Worcester. WR1 2JJ.
www.brownsrestaurant.co.uk
01905 26263.

The riverside location here is one of Brown's great attractions and the building is a stunner too, with an interior that is classy and serene.

A favourite haunt for years of local foodies, Brown's is now owned by Richard Everton (who also has Evertons deli, the Crown and Sandys and Kings Arms in Ombersley and the Hadley Bowling Green Inn). The interior has changed slightly, with bold patches of deep red breaking up the tranquil cream high walls.

The food is modern in style and decent quality with two menus on offer depending on how flush you feel.

Monsoon

Indian

35 Foregate Street, Worcester.
01905 726333.

The curry-lovers of Worcester are big fans of this modern, arty restaurant and the thoroughly indulgent food it offers.

It's not one for slimmers (is Indian food ever?) but ignore such considerations to make the most of its excellent menu.

Alongside the traditional favourites are some more unusual and tempting dishes such as dhaniya shorba (a soup), garlic jingah and daal panchmela.

The Quay Café Restaurant

Modern British

**Band House, South Quay,
Worcester, WR1 2JN.
www.thequayworcester.co.uk
01905 745792.**

Colourful, bright and breezy, the pretty Quay has a fab spot right by the river in the heart of Worcester.

It has a sunny cafe feel and does well for a daytime trade.

Evenings, it goes a bit more upmarket with a range of tried and tested dishes that offer bistro fare with a homely touch. Comfortable rather than cutting edge.

Saffron's Bistro

Modern British

**15 New Street, Worcester, WR1 2DP.
01905 610505.**

Bang in the centre of town but decidedly quaint, friendly Saffrons does a good range of bistro classics very well and to a thoroughly appreciative audience.

Flavours are richly satisfying and prices very reasonable.

VENUES BY CUISINE

Some places may appear in more than one category

American

Santa Fe

Bangladeshi

Bilash Tandoori, Wolverhampton
Cafes/bars
Apple Tree, Onibury
Arts Café, St Martins Church
Cafe Paxton, Paxton & Whitfield, Birmingham
Cafe@allsaints, Hereford
Daylesford Organic Farmshop Café, Daylesford
Dial cafe bar, Birmingham
French Connection, Stourbridge
Mortons, nr Solihull
Quay, Worcester

Caribbean

Xaymaca Experience

Chinese/Oriental

Cafe Soya, Birmingham
Cathay, Birmingham
China Red, Birmingham
Chung Ying, Birmingham
Chung Ying Garden, Birmingham
Henry Wong, Birmingham
Ruby Cantonese, Birmingham
Sobar, Birmingham
Tin Tin, Birmingham
Wing Wah, Oldbury
Wing Wah, Birmingham
Wong's, Birmingham
Yellow River, Solihull

English

Jonathans, Oldbury

Fine dining

De Vere Belfry, Sutton Coldfield
Brockencote Hall Hotel, Chaddesley Corbett
Buckland Manor, Buckland
Castle House Hotel, Hereford
Champignon Sauvage, Cheltenham
Colwall Park Hotel, Malvern
Corse Lawn House Hotel, nr Tewkesbury
Cotswold House Hotel (Garden Room restaurant), Chipping Campden
Cottage in the Wood, Malvern Wells
Elms, Abberley
Ettington Park Hotel, Alderminster
Fawsley Hall Hotel, Fawsley
Findons, Warwick
Four Seasons Restaurant at Swinfen Hall Hotel, nr Lichfield
Grafton Manor, Bromsgrove
Hambleton Hall, Hambleton
Hibiscus, Ludlow
Jessica's, Birmingham
Liaison, Birmingham
Lords of the Manor, Upper Slaughter
Lower Slaughter Manor, Lower Slaughter
Lygon Arms, Broadway
Mallory Court, Bishops Tachbrook, nr Leamington
Mr Underhill's, Ludlow
Nailcote Hall, Berkswell
New Hall Hotel, Sutton Coldfield
Nuthurst Grange, Hockley Heath
Paris, Birmingham
Restaurant Sat Bains, Nottingham
Russell's, Broadway
Simpsons, Birmingham
Welcombe Hotel, Stratford-upon-Avon
Wesley House, Winchcombe
Wood Norton Hall, Wood Norton, Evesham

Fish/seafood

Loch Fyne, Knowle

French

French Connection, Stourbridge
Hibiscus, Ludlow
Michelle's La Bastille, Birmingham
Oscar's at 39, Leamington Spa
Petit Blanc, Birmingham
Petit Blanc, Cheltenham
Restaurant Bosquet, Kenilworth
La Toque d'Or

Global

Azzari Too, Bearwood
Indi, Birmingham
Jam House, Birmingham

Indian

Al Frash, Birmingham
Barajee, Birmingham
Bilash Tandoori, Wolverhampton
Blue Mango, Birmingham
Cafe Lazeez, Birmingham
Coconut Lagoon, Birmingham
Coconut Lagoon, Stratford-upon-Avon
Itihaas, Birmingham
Jyoti, Birmingham
Lasan, Birmingham
Maharaja, Birmingham
Malabar, Birmingham
Mokhams, Birmingham
Monsoon, Worcester
Peppers, Birmingham
Rajdoot Tandoori, Birmingham
Rajnagar, Olton
Shimla Pinks, Birmingham
Ty's Jazz and Spice, Birmingham
Zafroni, Cannock

Indonesian

Indonesian, Studley

Italian

Buonissimo, Harborne, Birmingham
Cielo, Birmingham
Del Villaggio, Birmingham
Don Salvo, Birmingham
Fusion, Alcester Heath
Matricardi's, Henley-in-Arden
Milano, Birmingham
Tuscano, Stourbridge
Va Bene, Hagley
Valentinos, Harborne, Birmingham

Japanese

Shogun Sushi and Noodle Bar, Birmingham
Shogun Teppanyaki, Birmingham
Wagamama, Birmingham

Kashmiri

Ty's Jazz and Spice, Birmingham

Latin American

Las Iguanas, Birmingham
Santa Fe

Modern British

Apple Tree, Onibury
Aria, Hyatt Regency Hotel, Birmingham
Bank, Birmingham
Belle House, Pershore
Berlioz, Burlington Hotel, Birmingham
Bratz, Lichfield
Crowne Plaza Hotel, NEC, Birmingham
Brown's, Worcester
Cafe Paxton, Paxton & Whitfield, Birmingham
Cafe@allsaints, Hereford
Chandlers Grande Brasserie, Lichfield
City Café, City Inn, Birmingham
College of Food, Birmingham
Cotswold House Hotel (Hicks brasserie), Chipping Campden
Courtyard, Ludlow
Edmunds, Henley-in-Arden
Etcetera, Harborne, Birmingham
Findons, Warwick
Five North Street, Winchcombe
Floodgates Brasserie, Hereford
Fonteyns, Birmingham
Gallery Restaurant, Coventry
Goldies Brasserie, Birmingham
Haigs Hotel, Balsall Common
Hamiltons Brasserie, Stow-on-the-Wold
House of Fraser - Albert Roux restaurant, Birmingham
Hylton's, Banbury
Karibunis, Birmingham
Liaison, Birmingham
MacKenzie's, Birmingham
Malmaison, Birmingham
Matricardi's, Henley-in-Arden
McKees, Studley
Metro Bar and Grill, Birmingham
Metro Bar and Grill, Solihull
Mix at Mechu, Birmingham
Moat House Hotel, Acton Trussell
Mortons, Dickens Heath, nr Solihull
Mr Underhills, Ludlow
Noel Arms Hotel, Chipping Campden
Opposition, Stratford-upon-Avon

Opus, Birmingham
Paris, Birmingham
Pedmore House, Stourbridge
Pier 39, Sutton Coldfield
Prana Restaurant and Lounge, Birmingham
Quay, Worcester
Red Peppers, Birmingham
Restaurant Gilmore at Strine's Farm, nr Uttoxeter
Restaurant Sat Bains, Nottingham
Russell's, Broadway
Russons, Stratford-upon-Avon
Saffrons bistro, Worcester
Selfridges, Birmingham
Simply Simpsons, Kenilworth
Solo, Leamington Spa
Spirals, Knowle
Thrales, Lichfield
Venture In, Ombersley
Vintner, Stratford-upon-Avon
Waterdine, Llanfair Waterdine
Wesley House, Winchcombe
West 12, Birmingham
Zinc Bar and Grill, Birmingham

Modern European

Champignon Sauvage, Cheltenham
Chez Amis, Birmingham
Fusion, Alcester Heath
Hibiscus, Ludlow
Hotel du Vin, Birmingham
Jessica's, Birmingham
Simpsons, Birmingham
La Toque d'Or

Mongolian

Mongolian Bar, Birmingham

Moroccan

Zagora, Birmingham

Pakistani

Al Frash, Birmingham

Pubs/bars

Apres, Birmingham
Bar Epernay, Birmingham
Baraset Barn, Alveston
Barnt Green Inn
Bell and Cross, Clent
Bell, Alderminster
Bell, Tanworth-in-Arden
Bell, Welford-on-Avon
Boot Inn, Lapworth
Butchers Arms, Priors Hardwick
Chequers, Cutnall Green, nr Droitwich
Churchill Arms, Paxford
Cock at Wishaw, Sutton Coldfield
College Arms, nr Stratford-upon-Avon
Crabmill, Preston Bagot
Cross, Kenilworth
Cross Keys, Ombersley
Crown and Sandys, Ombersley
Crown at Iverley, Stourbridge
Dial cafe bar, Birmingham
Digress, Birmingham
Dominiques, Shatterford
Durham Ox, Shrewley
Ebrington Arms, nr Chipping Campden
Eight Bells Inn, Chipping Campden
Embargo, Stratford-upon-Avon
Etcetera, Birmingham
Fountain Inn, Clent
Fox and Goose, nr Stratford
Fox and Hounds, Great Wolford
Fox Inn, Stourton
Golden Cross, Ardens Grafton
Hadley Bowling Green Inn, nr Droitwich
Howard Arms, Ilmington
Jam House, Birmingham
King's Arms, Ombersley
King's Head, Aston Cantlow
Kings Arms, Stow-on-the-Wold
Living Room, Birmingham
Lloyds No 1, Lichfield
Loughpool Inn, Sellack
Lyttelton Arms, Hagley
Metro Bar and Grill, Birmingham
Metro Bar and Grill, Solihull
Mix at Mechu
Mortons Kitchen Bar and Deli, Dickens Heath, nr Solihull
Nailer's Arms, Bournheath
Oddfellows in the Boat, Lichfield
Old Chequers, Crowle

One Elm, Stratford-upon-Avon
Orange Tree, Chadwick End
Place 2B, Sutton Coldfield
Poppyred, Birmingham
Prana Restaurant and Lounge, Birmingham
Primitivo, Birmingham
Punchbowl, Lapworth
Queens, Belbroughton
Riverside Inn, Aymestrey
Roebuck, Brimfield
Rose and Crown, Warwick
Saint Pauls, Birmingham
Saxon Mill, Warwick
Seven Stars, Stourbridge
Stagg Inn, Titley
Talbot, Knightwick
Tarnished Halo, Birmingham
Three Crowns, Ullingswick
Waterdine, Llanfair Waterdine
West End, Stratford-upon-Avon
West One, Hagley
White Lion, Hampton-in-Arden
Wood, Rowington
Wykham Arms, Sibford Gower, nr Banbury
Zinc Bar and Grill, Birmingham

Spanish

Bar Estilo, Birmingham
Cafe Ikon, Birmingham
Chez Amis, Birmingham
La Tasca, Birmingham

Thai

Art Kitchen, Warwick
Barton Arms, Birmingham
Beau Thai, Solihull
Noel Arms Hotel, Chipping Campden
Thai Edge, Birmingham
Thai Orchid, Birmingham
Thai Rainbow, Lichfield

Vegetarian

Jyoti, Birmingham
Sibila's at Body and Being, Birmingham
Warehouse Café, Birmingham

VENUES BY COUNTY

Gloucestershire

Buckland Manor, Buckland
Champignon Sauvage, Cheltenham ★★
Churchill Arms, Paxford
Corse Lawn House Hotel, Corse Lawn, nr Tewkesbury ★
Cotswold House Hotel (Garden Room restaurant), Chipping Campden ★
Cotswold House Hotel (Hicks brasserie), Chipping Campden ★
Daylesford Organic Farmshop Café, Daylesford ★
Ebrington Arms, Ebrington, Chipping Campden
Eight Bells Inn, Chipping Campden
Five North Street, Winchcombe ★
Hamiltons Brasserie, Stow-on-the-Wold
Kings Arms, Stow-on-the-Wold
Lords of the Manor, Upper Slaughter ★★
Lower Slaughter Manor, Lower Slaughter
Noel Arms Hotel, Chipping Campden ★
Wesley House, Winchcombe ★

Herefordshire

Cafe@allsaints, Hereford
Castle House Hotel, Hereford ★
Floodgates Brasserie, Hereford
Loughpool Inn, Sellack
Riverside Inn, Aymestrey
Stagg Inn, Titley ★
Three Crowns, Ullingswick ★

Northamptonshire

Fawsley Hall Hotel, Fawsley

Nottinghamshire

Restaurant Sat Bains, Nottingham ★★

Oxon

Hylton's, Banbury
Wykham Arms, Sibford Gower, nr Banbury ★

Rutland

Hambleton Hall, Hambleton

Shropshire

Apple Tree, Onibury
Courtyard, Ludlow
Hibiscus, Ludlow ★★
Mr Underhills, Ludlow ★★
Roebuck, Brimfield
Waterdine, Llanfair Waterdine ★

Staffordshire

Bratz, Lichfield
Chandlers Grande Brasserie, Lichfield
Four Seasons Restaurant at Swinfen Hall Hotel, Swinfen, nr Lichfield
Lloyds No 1, Lichfield
Moat House Hotel, Acton Trussell
Oddfellows in the Boat, Lichfield
Restaurant Gilmore at Strine's Farm, Beamhurst, Uttoxeter ★
Thai Rainbow, Lichfield
Thrales, Lichfield
Zafroni, Cannock

Warwickshire

Art Kitchen, Warwick ★
Baraset Barn, Alveston, nr Stratford ★
Bell, Alderminster
Bell, Tanworth-in-Arden ★
Bell, Welford-on-Avon
Boot Inn, Lapworth
Butchers Arms, Priors Hardwick
Coconut Lagoon, Stratford-upon-Avon
College Arms, Lower Quinton, Stratford-upon-Avon ★
Crabmill, Preston Bagot
Cross, Kenilworth
Durham Ox, Shrewley
Edmunds, Henley-in-Arden ★★
Embargo, Stratford-upon-Avon
Ettington Park Hotel, Alderminster
Findons, Warwick
Fox and Goose, Armscote, nr Stratford
Fox and Hounds, Great Wolford
Fusion, Alcester Heath
Gallery Restaurant, Coventry
Golden Cross, Ardens Grafton
Haigs Hotel, Balsall Common
Howard Arms, Ilmington ★
Indonesian, Studley
King's Head, Aston Cantlow
Mallory Court, Bishops Tachbrook, nr Leamington ★
Matricardi's, Henley-in-Arden ★
McKees, Studley

Nailcote Hall, Berkswell
Nuthurst Grange, Hockley Heath
One Elm, Stratford-upon-Avon
Opposition, Stratford-upon-Avon
Orange Tree, Chadwick End
Oscar's at 39, Leamington Spa
Punchbowl, Lapworth
Restaurant Bosquet, Kenilworth ★
Rose and Crown, Warwick
Russons, Stratford-upon-Avon
Saxon Mill, Warwick
Simply Simpsons, Kenilworth ★
Solo, Leamington Spa ★
Vintner, Stratford-upon-Avon
Welcombe Hotel, Stratford-upon-Avon
West End, Stratford-upon-Avon
White Lion, Hampton-in-Arden
Wood, Rowington ★

West Midlands

Al Frash, Birmingham
Apres, Birmingham
Aria restaurant at Hyatt Regency Hotel, Birmingham
Arts Cafe, St Martins Church, Birmingham
Azzari Too, Bearwood
Bank, Birmingham ★
Bar Epernay, Birmingham
Bar Estilo, Birmingham
Barajee, Birmingham
Barnt Green Inn, Barnt Green
Barton Arms, Aston, Birmingham
Beau Thai, Solihull
Belfry, Wishaw, Sutton Coldfield
Berlioz, Burlington Hotel, Birmingham
Bilash Tandoori, Wolverhampton ★ ★
Blue Mango, Birmingham
Crowne Plaza Hotel, NEC, Birmingham
Buonissimo, Harborne, Birmingham
Cafe Ikon, Birmingham
Cafe Lazeez, Birmingham
Cafe Paxton, Paxton & Whitfield, Birmingham
Cafe Soya, Birmingham
Cathay, Birmingham
Chez Amis, Birmingham
China Red, Birmingham
Chung Ying, Birmingham
Chung Ying Garden, Birmingham
Cielo, Birmingham
City Café, City Inn, Birmingham
Cock at Wishaw, Sutton Coldfield

Coconut Lagoon, Birmingham
College of Food, Birmingham
Crown at Iverley, Stourbridge
Del Villaggio, Birmingham
Denial, Birmingham
Dial cafe bar, Birmingham
Digress, Birmingham
Don Salvo, Birmingham
Etcetera, Harborne, Birmingham
Fonteyns, Birmingham
Fountain Inn, Clent
Fox Inn, Stourton
French Connection, Stourbridge
Goldies Brasserie, Birmingham
Henry Wong, Birmingham
Hotel du Vin, Birmingham
House of Fraser - Albert Roux restaurant, Birmingham
Indi, Birmingham
Itihaas, Birmingham
Jam House, Birmingham
Jessica's, Birmingham ★ ★
Jonathans, Oldbury
Jyoti, Birmingham
Karibunis, Birmingham
La Tasca, Birmingham
Las Iguanas, Birmingham
Lasan, Birmingham ★
Liaison, Birmingham
Living Room, Birmingham
Locanta Piccalilli Birmingham
Loch Fyne, Knowle
MacKenzie's Bar and Dining Room, Birmingham ★
Maharaja, Birmingham
Malabar, Birmingham
Malmaison, Birmingham ★
Metro Bar and Grill, Birmingham
Metro Bar and Grill, Solihull
Michelle's La Bastille, Birmingham
Milano, Birmingham
Mix at Mechu, Birmingham ★
Mokhams, Birmingham
Mongolian Bar, Birmingham
Mortons Kitchen Bar and Deli, Dickens Heath, nr Solihull ★
New Hall Hotel, Sutton Coldfield
Opus, Birmingham ★
Paris, Birmingham ★
Pedmore House, Stourbridge
Peppers, Birmingham
Petit Blanc, Birmingham
Petit Blanc, Cheltenham
Pier 39, Sutton Coldfield

Place 2B, Sutton Coldfield
Poppyred, Birmingham
Prana Restaurant and Lounge, Birmingham ★
Primitivo, Birmingham
Rajdoot Tandoori, Birmingham
Rajnagar, Olton
Red Peppers, Birmingham
Ruby Cantonese, Birmingham
Saint Pauls, Birmingham
Santa Fe, Birmingham
Selfridges, Birmingham ★
Seven Stars, Stourbridge
Shimla Pinks, Birmingham
Shogun Sushi and Noodle Bar, Birmingham
Shogun Teppanyaki, Birmingham
Sibila's at Body and Being, Birmingham
Simpsons, Birmingham ★ ★
Sobar, Birmingham
Spirals, Knowle
Tarnished Halo, Birmingham
Thai Edge, Birmingham
Thai Orchid, Birmingham
Tin Tin, Birmingham
Toque d'Or, Birmingham ★
Tuscano, Stourbridge
Ty's Jazz and Spice, Birmingham
Valentinos, Harborne, Birmingham
Wagamama, Birmingham
Warehouse Café, Birmingham
West 12, Birmingham
Wing Wah, Oldbury
Wing Wah, Birmingham
Wong's, Birmingham ★
Xaymaca Experience, Birmingham
Yellow River, Solihull
Zagora, Birmingham
Zinc Bar and Grill, Birmingham

Worcestershire

Bell and Cross, Clent ★
Belle House, Pershore ★
Brockencote Hall Hotel, Chaddesley Corbett ★
Brown's, Worcester
Chequers, Cutnall Green, nr Droitwich ★
Colwall Park Hotel, Colwall, Malvern
Cottage in the Wood, Malvern Wells
Cross Keys, Ombersley
Crown and Sandys, Ombersley
Dominiques, Shatterford
Elms, Abberley ★

Grafton Manor, Bromsgrove
Hadley Bowling Green Inn, Hadley Heath, nr Droitwich
King's Arms, Ombersley
Lygon Arms, Broadway
Lyttelton Arms, Hagley
Monsoon, Worcester
Nailer's Arms, Bournheath
Old Chequers, Crowle
Quay, Worcester
Queens, Belbroughton
Russell's, Broadway
Saffrons bistro, Worcester
Talbot, Knightwick
Va Bene, Hagley
Venture In, Ombersley ★
West One, Hagley
Wood Norton Hall, Wood Norton, Evesham

INDEX

INDEX

Le Champignon Sauvage

£5 off

lunch Tuesday to Saturday.

Suffolk Road, Cheltenham, GL50 2AQ. 01242 573449

Only one voucher to be used per transaction. To be used by August 31, 2006.
Photocopies will not be accepted

Simpsons

£5 off

lunch or dinner Monday to Thursday inclusive.

20 Highfield Road, Edgbaston, Birmingham, B15. 0121 454 3434.

Only one voucher to be used per transaction. To be used by August 31, 2006.
Photocopies will not be accepted

Jessica's

£5 off

any meal Tuesday to Thursday inclusive.

1 Montague Road, Edgbaston, Birmingham, B16 9HN. 0121 455 0999.

Only one voucher to be used per transaction. To be used by August 31, 2006.
Photocopies will not be accepted

Opus

£5 off

any meal any day.

54 Cornwall Street, Birmingham, B3 2DE. 0121 200 2323.

Only one voucher to be used per transaction. To be used by August 31, 2006.
Photocopies will not be accepted

Baraset Barn, Alveston; **the Boot** at Lapworth; **the Crabmill**, Preston Bagot; **Orange Tree**, Chadwick End; **Mortons**, Dickens Heath, Solihull; **Saxon Mill**, Warwick; **Barnt Green Inn**, Barnt Green; **Cock at Wishaw**, nr Sutton Coldfield; **Lyttelton Arms**, Hagley, nr Stourbridge.

£5 off

any meal Monday-Wednesday inclusive.

Only one voucher to be used per transaction. To be used by August 31, 2006.
Photocopies will not be accepted

EATING OUT
IN BIRMINGHAM AND THE MIDLANDS
MONEY OFF VOUCHERS

Photocopies not accepted.

Only one voucher to be used per transaction.

To be used by August 31, 2006.

EATING OUT
IN BIRMINGHAM AND THE MIDLANDS
MONEY OFF VOUCHERS

Photocopies not accepted.

Only one voucher to be used per transaction.

To be used by August 31, 2006.

EATING OUT
IN BIRMINGHAM AND THE MIDLANDS
MONEY OFF VOUCHERS

Photocopies not accepted.

Only one voucher to be used per transaction.

To be used by August 31, 2006.

EATING OUT
IN BIRMINGHAM AND THE MIDLANDS
MONEY OFF VOUCHERS

Photocopies not accepted.

Only one voucher to be used per transaction.

To be used by August 31, 2006.

EATING OUT
IN BIRMINGHAM AND THE MIDLANDS
MONEY OFF VOUCHERS

Photocopies not accepted.

Only one voucher to be used per transaction.

To be used by August 31, 2006.

Alison Davison is not half as fat as you might think, despite having been The Birmingham Post's restaurant critic and writer/editor of its eating out guide since April 1997. She also has an online restaurant guide, www.eat-the-midlands.co.uk, and edits Foodie magazine, a publication dedicated to food and drink in the Midlands (www.thefoodie.co.uk).

She is a former inspector for the Good Food Guide and judge at the British Cheese Awards.

Alison was born in Wigan and graduated with an honours degree in English literature from Sheffield University. She has two children, lives in Worcestershire and likes to spend the small hours worrying needlessly.